Q —

Ray, how many questions do you get for *Fix It Friday*?

A —

An average of 2,000 during Friday's show and another 1,500 related texts and emails during the week.

Foreword

There you are. You've bought the book or maybe got it as a present, either way you're reading the foreword. I'm impressed, not everybody reads forewords. Thanks!

You may be slightly interested in the fact that a lot of folk ask me about the origins of *Fix It Friday*. Firstly, let me say that if we knew it was going to be so successful we would have named it differently, don't ask me what!

Its genesis was truly organic, as organic as roughage actually. It all started with an innocent textual query (sounds pervy) about the lyrics to an old TV advertisement: 'You know that ad, Ray, "They're tasty, tasty, very very tasty . . ." What did it advertise and what was the rest of the song?'

We got the answer for the perplexed and slightly sad listener and then before you could text the words 'This has been wrecking my head', we were providing an informal fact-finding service. The listeners asked; we answered – quite straightforward. Then Martin, Jenny or Ray, depending on which version of the story you believe, dreamt up the wonderfully simple idea of *Fix It Friday*. Because of the alliteration I suspect it was me (alliteration being a nasty affliction, which besets children's television presenters).

Anyway, that's how it all started and since its inception we have received hundreds of thousands of texts about a myriad of topics from the insignificant to the monumental.

What is contained here is only a small fraction of the questions and the answers. We would hope that they are representative of the hugely interesting questions that irk our listeners.

We have done our damnedest to deliver definitive answers (always with the alliteration!) however we may have failed the odd time. That's a nice way of issuing a disclaimer about the information contained between these covers. Enjoy!

I say thank-you mór to Martin Maguire 'The Mountain of Knowledge'; *Fix It Friday* help desk babe, Jenny Kelly ably assisted by Mairead Farrell; to all at Mentor Books including Nicola, Claire and Boss-man Danny; to all at Today FM especially Boss-man Willie; to Aidan and Brian in the music department and to Adelle.

Special thanks to all those people who have shared their expert knowledge with us. And biggest of big thank-you mór to the listeners of *The Ray D'Arcy Show* – truly special people!

Off you go now and read the book. By the way, I'm not spoiling it for you when I tell you there's a 'Happy Ending'!

Ray D'Arcy

Contents

THE BODY

How does an insomniac meet the girl of his dreams? — *Anon*

Is acupuncture any good for pins and needles? — *Mary*

Why do women remember everything? — *John, Dublin*

Q —

Why do men have nipples?

A —

After conception the developing foetus does not display any sex differences. It is impossible to determine from a scan whether the developing foetus is male or female until after approximately 14 weeks when the male and female hormones are produced and dictate the development of male or female body features.

However, prior to the arrival of testosterone (the male hormone), the foetus had been happily developing nipples. If the foetus is female the presence of oestrogen and progestorone lead ultimately to the development of the nipples into glands in the grown female. On the other hand, if the foetus is male the presence of testosterone prevents further development of the nipples – they remain as constant reminders that we all start off the same!

Q —

Ray, can you tell me if it takes more muscles to frown than to smile?

A —

It takes as few as two muscles to produce a smile and as few as three to give a frown.

Q —

Is it true that you can't keep your eyes open when you sneeze?

A —

For what appears to be a simple act the sneeze is quite complicated. Here's the science. A sneeze occurs when the nerve endings of the mucous membrane of the nose are irritated. This irritation then stimulates your trigeminal nerve, sending impulses to a set of neurons located in the brainstem that have collectively been termed the 'sneezing centre'.

The sneezing centre then sends new impulses along the facial nerve back to the nasal passages and the face, causing your nasal passages to secrete fluid and become congested. (The 'nasal phase' of the sneeze.) Your eyes may also water. At the same time, the sneezing centre also sends impulses to your respiratory muscles via the spinal cord. It is these impulses that create the deep inbreath and forceful outbreath (the 'respiratory phase') that we know as the sneeze.

So why do our eyes always shut at the moment of sneezing? The reason for this is simply that the impulses travelling through the facial nerve, as mentioned above, also happen to stimulate nerves which govern the reflex response we call the blink. So, essentially, one message is sent, but two listeners receive it, and act on it. Hence the sneeze–blink. So no, you can't keep your eyes open when you sneeze.

Q —

Why do we get goosebumps when we are cold?

A —

Goosebumps are caused by a contraction of miniature muscles that are attached to each hair. Each contracting muscle creates a shallow depression on the skin surface, which causes the surrounding area to protrude. The contraction also causes the hair to stand up whenever the body feels cold. In animals with a thick hair coat this rising of hair expands the layer of air that serves as insulation. The thicker the hair layer, the more heat is retained. In people this reaction is useless because we do not have a hair coat, but is a leftover from our ancestors who were hairier than we are today.

In addition to cold, the hair will also stand up in many animals when they feel threatened. People also tend to experience goosebumps during emotional situations, such as walking down the aisle during their wedding or even simply remembering an emotional event. The reason for these responses is the subconscious release of a stress hormone called adrenaline. In humans, adrenaline is often released when we feel cold or afraid, but also if we are under stress and feel strong emotions, such as anger or excitement.

Q —

Can you tell us why our fingers wrinkle in the bath?

A —

The component parts of the epidermis (outer layer of the skin) absorb water at different rates and therefore expand at different rates. The outer part expands more than the inner part, thus the skin wrinkles like a gathered skirt.

Q —

Why do our brains look like walnuts? Is there a reason for the convoluted surface?

A —

The human brain is a very efficient use of space! Much of the brain's work is carried out in the top few layers of cells. The fissures in the brain increase its surface area without the need for a larger skull diameter. Less smart animals, rats for example, have a smooth brain surface.

Q —

What causes the big black bags under your eyes when you're really tired?

A —

There can be a number of causes for dark circles under the eyes. Iron deficiency is one possibility. Another is an allergy or other problem affecting your liver or kidneys. Poor dietary habits or excessive consumption of alcohol can affect the functions of these organs. People who increase their daily intake of water and eat plenty of raw fruit and vegetables usually see their black bags disappear!

Q —

Why do we have a philtrum, you know, the groove above your mouth?

A —

Well, children use it to store snot until a grown-up arrives with a tissue! For adults, it serves no purpose at all. It is one of a number of merger-lines in the body known as raphes. As the embryo develops, the right and left sides merge at various points on the body, resulting in a raphe. Similar meeting points can be found in the middle of your tongue, in the dent under your chin and in some other unmentionable places!

Q —

What is the global mortality rate per minute?

A —

What a question! The answer is that approximately 100 people 'shuffle off this mortal coil' every sixty seconds but, in the same time, about 250 are taking their first breath. Therefore the net increase in the population of the planet is roughly 150 souls per minute.

Q —

Why does my eye twitch?

A —

The medical name for this common phenomenon is ocular myokymia. It is often associated with fatigue. Other causes can be too much caffeine or increased stress. It is almost always temporary and completely harmless and, although the sensation is very noticeable to you, your twitching eye is not visible to anyone else.

Q —

Do twins have the same DNA?

A —

There are two kinds of twins, fraternal and identical. Fraternal twins develop from two independently fertilised eggs and their DNA is different. Identical twins develop from a single fertilised egg, known as a zygote, which splits into two cell clusters, each of which eventually becomes a separate human being. Since there was only one complete set of DNA in the zygote, there is only one set at the end of the process and the identical twins have the same DNA.

Q —

Why can't you taste anything when your nose is blocked?

A —

Well, don't blame your taste buds as they only do about 25 percent of the work at the best of times, distinguishing only between bitter, salty, sweet and sour flavours. About 75 percent of what we perceive as taste comes from our sense of smell. When you put food into your mouth, odour molecules travel through the passage between your nose and mouth to olfactory receptor cells at the top of your nasal cavity. If mucus in your nasal passages is too thick, air and odour molecules can't reach these smell receptors, then your brain receives no signal from which to identify the odour. Thus, when you are 'bunged up', everything you eat and drink tastes much the same.

Q —

Do the 32 teeth in your head include your wisdom teeth?

A —

Yes. The average adult has 32 teeth, each with a specific name and function. The teeth we know as wisdom teeth are properly called your third molars. These are the last teeth to erupt and sometimes they are just four teeth too many as the modern human jaw often accommodates 28 teeth more comfortably than 32!

Q —

How many bones are in the human body?

A —

An adult human skeleton contains 206 bones, more than half of them in your hands and feet. As we all know from the milk advertisements, a child's skeleton contains more – over 300, many of which fuse together as he or she grows.

Q —

Why do farts smell so bad?

A —

It all happens in your large intestine. Billions of bacteria attack undigested food. As the food is broken down a variety of gases are produced, including methane, hydrogen and hydrogen sulphide. The gas with the offensive odour is hydrogen sulphide. Certain foods produce more flatulence than others because they contain indigestible carbohydrates which pass through the stomach and small intestine in a relatively undigested state, giving all those bacteria in the large intestine plenty of work. A prime example of such a food is 'the musical fruit', the baked bean!

Q —

Do women have Adam's apples?

A —

Yes. The Adam's apple is the outer part of the voice box or larynx. It enlarges in boys during puberty and male larynx muscles are much stronger than women's, hence their deeper voices.

Q —

Why do we have eyebrows?

A —

Nobody is entirely sure why we still have this particular facial hair but it is probably to keep moisture out of our eyes when we sweat or are out in the rain. The arched shape of the eyebrow diverts the moisture to the sides of the face, keeping our eyes relatively dry. This is particularly useful in the case of sweat, which is salty and would sting the eyes.

Q —

Is it true that it takes seven years for chewing gum to pass through your body if you swallow it?

A —

No. Chewing gum is eliminated from the body at the same rate as any other swallowed matter. However, it is indigestible and will re-emerge in more or less the same condition as it entered your system. Yuk!

Q —

What is the purpose of snot?

A —

Your nose produces a lot of this stuff every day – about a coffee cup full! Snot is very useful, trapping germs, dirt, pollen and bacteria in your nose and preventing them from getting to your lungs.

Q —

How long can hair grow?

A —

Very long indeed. In 1998 an 85-year-old man in Thailand, Mr Hook, had his hair measured at an amazing 5.24 metres – beat that!

Q —

How come you don't sneeze while sleeping?

A —

It is possible to sneeze in your sleep if the stimulus is strong enough, however it is unusual. Sneezing is a reflex response to stimulus in your nasal mucus and this stimulus has to reach your brainstem centre before the brain's neurons can trigger a response. Because brain activity declines during sleep, this stimulus will not generally reach the brainstem centre to promote the normal waking response.

Q —

Why can't we tickle ourselves?

A —

This is a question that has irked many scientific minds. The brief but complicated psycho physiological answer is, when a movement is self produced, its sensory consequences can be accurately predicted and this prediction can be used to attenuate the sensory effects of the movement. In other words you know the what, when and where of the tickle and you are in complete control of what happens thus the surprise and unpredictable elements which are essential to a good tickle are not present.

Q —

How long does hair take to grow?

A —

Hair grows at about one centimetre a month. Your hair would take about three years to grow to shoulder-length. However, if you want it down to your waist you'll have to wait about seven years.

Q —

Where do warts come from?

A —

Warts are non-cancerous skin growths caused by the human papilloma virus (HPV). There are several different types of warts, including common wart, flat wart and plantar wart (also known as a verruca).

Q —

What makes fingernails?

A —

Nails are made from protein fibres, specifically the protein keratin. The essential building blocks have to come from plants, as proteins are made from amino acids which animals (including humans) cannot make for themselves. We acquire these vital ingredients by consuming plants or another animal which has eaten plants. Human nails are made from the same material as horse hooves, bird talons and feathers, and hair.

Q —

Why do you get tears in your eyes when you yawn?

A —

In the corner of each eye is a lachrymal sac, which holds tear fluid. When you yawn your facial muscles squeeze these sacs and a small amount of tear fluid is discharged.

Q —

Ray and the gang. What do people who've been blind from birth dream about? I've always wondered, because if they've never seen anything, how can they dream?

— *Val, Letterkenny*

To answer this we talked to Emer Mulhall, who was the IT Tutor at the National Council for the Blind of Ireland.

A —

Well Ray, I've been asked that question many times before so what I would really say is that I dream the same way as many other people do, in that I dream about something that has happened to me or an experience or an event. The difference is any sensations would be either audible or tactile. For example, I dreamt recently about a car crash and I have been involved in a minor car crash. In my dream, I could feel the car swerving and I could hear the noise of the glass breaking and the metal crunching. It was actually quite frightening, I suppose – you could call it a nightmare really! And then in my dream, I actually put my hand on somebody's hand that had a little cut, not badly injured but a small cut. So I got the sensation of touch in that way within the dream. It was all pretty frightening at the time but I would have dreams too where by I would just be running or walking through a field. Whatever I'm doing in the dream would have to involve somebody talking to me or I was doing something or I would be touching something. It wouldn't be visual images because I've never seen anything and I have nothing in my brain to say 'that's what a table looks like' or 'that's what a television looks like'. I'd never be watching a television programme in my dream but I'd be listening!

ANIMALS

'Curiosity' was the dog's name. — *Anon*

Stop the press! A dog breeder in Cavan has just come up with a Doberman–Labrador hybrid. It frightens the shite out of you and then brings you the toilet roll. — *Monaghan listener*

Why don't sheep shrink when it rains?
— *Julie, Wicklow*

Q —

Could you please tell me what the biggest cat in the world is? Now not pet cats, I mean wild cats.

A —

The Siberian tiger, whose scientific name is *Panthera tigris altaica*, is the world's largest cat. Males can grow to 4 metres in length and weigh up to 300kg! The numbers of Siberian tigers in the wild are dangerously low but they are still found in eastern Russia, north-eastern China and the northern extremes of North Korea.

Q —

Why do birds tend to fly in a V-shape?

A —

The V-shape formation is very aerodynamic, reducing air resistance. This allows migrating birds to glide for longer, thus conserving energy, and to cover greater distances. In fact, a flock of geese using this formation can fly 70% further than a solo bird. Other benefits include an unobstructed field of vision for each bird and an opportunity for a tired leader to drop back into the formation while another bird takes the front.

Q —

Hi, what is a male swan called and can they break your arm with a smack of their wing?

A —

A male swan is called a cob (the female is a pen and a young swan is a cygnet). Swans are bright birds! They can remember individual people and will recall who was nice to them and who gave them grief. They do not attack for food but will defend vigorously their territory, nest or young. Swans usually attack with their wings, which are extremely strong and can cause serious injury, especially to children. Regarding their potential to break arms, I'd recommend that you don't get close enough to find out!

Q —

Do insects sleep? Is it true that all living things need sleep?

A —

It is believed that most insects do not sleep. However, the exception to this is honey bees. They do enter a state of profound rest at night when movement, muscle tone, body temperature and sensitivity to stimuli are all reduced. Even in the twenty-first century the function of sleep in birds and mammals (including humans) is not completely understood. It is thought that it gives our bodies time to do essential repair and maintenance and perhaps to do some memory processing. Creatures with very tiny brains, such as insects, appear to have no need of sleep.

Q —

Ray, could you tell me what the horns on the head of a giraffe are for?

A —

The giraffe's 'horns' are not real horns at all. They are bony lumps on the skull covered with skin and hair. Their scientific name is ossicones. Males usually have larger ossicones than females and more of them too, sometimes as many as five. Mature males use these bony lumps when fighting and the hair on top of them is gradually rubbed away.

Q —

Ray, please please answer me this . . . What do you call a group of rabbits? Please I need to know it's wreckin' my head.

A —

Spare your head. A group of rabbits is called a herd.

Q —

I'm travelling to Australia in 20 days time and I've heard some horrific stories of funnel web spiders hidden in toilet seats. Is it true? I'm very afraid. HELP!

A —

Don't believe everything you hear. Australian funnel web spiders are indeed highly venomous. The most feared of the species is the Sydney funnel web, *Atrax Robustus*. When disturbed or annoyed the spider produces a poison droplet from the tip of its fangs. The venom of the male is more toxic than that of the female. There is severe pain at the site of the bite and the victim may experience excessive sweating, vomiting and a rapid rise in blood pressure. Coma or respiratory obstruction sometimes occur. The legends about funnel web spiders lying in wait under toilet seats originate from outdoor toilets in wooden shacks. These shacks would be warm and dark – ideal spider habitat!

Q —

What's the difference between a turtle and a tortoise?

A —

Turtles, tortoises and terrapins are all members of the Testudine family. The main difference between the turtle and the tortoise is that turtles are both land and water-dwelling, whereas tortoises are land-dwelling only.

Q —

We all know birds poo because we can see it on our cars but do they pee as well or is it mixed together?

A —

Birds excrete nitrogenous wastes in the form of uric acid, rather than urea as mammals do. Unlike urea, uric acid is almost insoluble in water and is excreted in the form of crystals that form a semisolid white paste called urates. Bird droppings usually contain both white urates and a concentrated mass of digestive wastes such as insect cuticle and seeds. In other words, they are mixed together.

Which end of an egg comes out first, the big end or the small end? Please give us an answer.

Chickens, as well as other birds, have a common opening for reproduction and the evacuation of stools and urine. The intestine, ureters and oviduct come together into a common chamber called the cloaca. As you would expect, this is a somewhat dirty place but the clever hen manages to lay eggs which are perfectly clean and virtually sterile. This is achieved by turning part of the cloaca and the last segment of the oviduct inside out. Thus the egg emerges uncontaminated, sometimes with the rounded end first and sometimes with the pointed end first!

What is a young turkey called?

A —

A poult.

Q —

Ray, how do pigeons find their way home?

A —

The process by which migrating birds navigate is fairly well understood. They possess a 'compass sense' and navigate in daytime using the sun. They also have a 'magnetic sense' which allows them to locate North and thereby navigate on cloudy days. However, a homing pigeon requires an additional skill in order to determine its starting point for its homeward journey – it needs a sense of location or 'map sense'.

An extraordinary event over the English Channel in 1997 gave a possible explanation of how pigeons navigate. On 29th June, at 6.30am, sixty thousand homing pigeons were released from a field in Nantes (northern France), destined for lofts all over the South of England 640 to 800 kilometres away. By 11.00am most of the birds were over the Channel. At the same time the Paris-to-New York Concorde was flying above the Channel and generating its famous 'sonic boom', a gigantic shock wave which creates a carpet of sound 150 kilometres wide. The majority of the birds would have been in the path of this intense wave of sound.

The birds were expected home early that afternoon but none arrived. A few thousand stragglers arrived over the next few days but most of the pigeons were never seen again. It is believed that homing pigeons use atmospheric infrasounds when navigating. These are very low frequency sounds which travel thousands of kilometres from their source (this is how we hear the roll of distant thunder). The pigeon's ear is remarkably good at detecting very low frequency sounds. Such a low frequency sound that would be audible to pigeons all over the world is the acoustic shock generated by ocean waves crashing against one another. When these sounds are reflected off cliffs, mountains or other steep-sided features on the earth's surface they can provide the bird with a detailed 'sound picture' of its surroundings.

It is believed that what happened in the great homing pigeon disaster of 1997 was that the huge wave of infrasound generated by Concorde obliterated the normal oceanic shockwave information which the birds were relying on, completely disorientating them. Thus it was only the slower birds, those who missed the passing of the supersonic plane, who finally made it home.

Q —

How do I attract hedgehogs into my garden?

A —

Hedgehogs are useful in the garden because they eat slugs and other garden pests. However, wild hedgehogs are protected by EU Directives and cannot be taken from their natural habitats. If you want to encourage hedgehogs into your garden, avoid the use of pesticides and insecticides – these will kill the hedgehog as well as the bugs you're trying to get rid of. Do not feed them bread and milk (as is often done) as this will make them sick – dog food is much better!

(Answer kindly supplied by Wild Ireland Magazine)

Q —

What do seals drink?

A —

Most seals get their water from the foods they eat. However, female seals have been known to eat snow when they are lactating (giving milk to their young) and their food intake is reduced.

Q —

How long does it take for a frog to develop from spawn?

A —

About six weeks after the tadpole hatches from the spawn, little legs start to appear, shortly followed by arms. The head becomes more distinct and the body lengthens. By about nine weeks the tadpole begins to look like a frog with a tail. By the twelfth week the tail has regressed, and between twelve and sixteen weeks the tadpole has evolved into a frog.

Q —

How many inches in a hand – as in horse?

A —

One hand is equal to four inches (10 centimetres). The reason for this is that, traditionally, horses were measured using the width of a person's hand, which is approximately four inches. A horse is measured from the ground to its shoulder. The most accurate measurement is obtained by means of a measuring stick. This is a large wooden 'ruler' marked in hands with another piece of wood at right angles which can be lowered onto the horse's withers (the ridge between the shoulder blades).

Q —

Why do killer whales' fins fall to one side when in captivity?

A —

The dorsal fin of adult male killer whales is tall. In its natural environment a healthy whale swims a lot, often at high speed and usually in a straight line. This activity helps the large dorsal fin to maintain its shape. However, in captivity they do not swim as much and never at high speed, nor can they swim in a straight line for any great distance. This lack of exercise causes the connective tissue supporting the dorsal fin to waste away and eventually its own weight causes it to fall over.

Q —

Do ostriches stick their heads in the sand?

A —

Not really, but an ostrich will lower its head towards the ground if it senses danger, especially when it is sitting on a nest. Also, males ostriches use their bills to dig shallow nests in the sand and move their eggs around. From a distance this could be mistaken for the bird burying its head in the sand!

Q —

What was the name of the Russian mutt that went to space?

A —

The mutt's name was Laika and she was launched into space in *Sputnik 2* on 3rd November 1957. Her real name was Kudryavka (meaning Little Curly) but because she was part husky she came to be known as Laika, which is Russian for husky. She was the first living creature to be launched into orbit. She survived only a few hours into the flight, probably dying from overheating, fear and stress. Laika was the only animal Russian scientists knowingly sent into space to die – she would certainly not have survived re-entry to the Earth's atmosphere.

Q —

Do penguins have knees?

A —

They sure do, although they are discreetly hidden underneath their feathers. Penguins, like other birds, have legs divided into three segments. The upper segment, the equivalent of our thigh, and the middle segment, the equivalent of our shinbone or the drumstick of a chicken, are both quite short in penguins. So penguins, do have knees, with patellas (knee caps) that bend and function much like their human counterparts.

Q —

Where do badgers live?

A —

Badgers live in family groups in a set. The set is a maze of underground chambers and tunnels which can exist for hundreds of years if undisturbed by human activity.

Q —

Is it true that pigeons secrete milk?

A —

Yes, like mammals, some young birds are fed on secretions from their parents. Unlike mammals, both male and female birds produce these secretions, the best known example being the pigeon. Adult pigeons feed their young (called squabs) with crop milk. This is secreted from fluid-filled cells in the lining of the crop, a digestive pouch which protrudes from the bottom of the oesophagus. Crop milk contains more fat and protein than either cow or human milk and is fed to the squabs for at least two weeks after hatching.

Q —

Is it true that horses cannot vomit?

A —

Both horses and humans have a band of muscle around the bottom of the oesophagus, where it enters the stomach. This operates as a one-way valve to prevent food and stomach secretions from re-entering the oesophagus. The difference is that in horses it is truly effective! If a human has a digestive problem, vomiting may be the answer, but this is not an option for a horse. In addition to the extremely efficient cut-off valve, the angle at which the oesophagus meets the stomach is such that any bloating tends to enhance the one-way function and prevent food from being regurgitated. This can have dire consequences for the horse as severe bloating will usually cause the stomach to rupture before the valve gives way.

Q —

Is one year of a dog's life really equal to seven human years?

A —

This is the generally accepted rough guide to the human equivalent of a dog's age. However, it does not recognise the fact that dogs reach maturity within about two years. A more accurate formula to assess your dog's age in human terms is to allow 10.5 dog years per human year for the first two years and then four dog years for each subsequent human year, for example, if your dog is five years old that is equivalent to 33 human years.

Q —

I've just been bitten all over by midges – are they a type of mosquito?

A —

Midges and mosquitoes are both varieties of gnat. The midge is a tiny dipterous (two-winged) fly and there are thousands of species, most of which are completely harmless. However, the ones which do feed off humans are well-equipped to do so, possessing two finely toothed mandibles and a maxilla. (That's a lot of biting and chewing power for something you can barely see!) They detect their victims by body odour and possibly breath.

Q —

Is there such an animal as a zeedonk?

A —

The first recorded zeedonks were the result of an unintended mating between a male Chapman's zebra and a female black ass (donkey) at Colchester Zoo in England in 1983. The mating was successful because the zebra and the donkey belong to the same genus, *Equus*. Such cross-breeding between different species of the same genus results in a hybrid which is invariably sterile; therefore zeedonks cannot reproduce. Such cross-species matings are not encouraged in modern zoos.

Q —

If a turtle has no shell, is he homeless or naked?

A —

Perhaps he's just a lizard!

Q —

How long are elephants pregnant – mine looks well overdue!

A —

The gestation period for an elephant is 22 months. They do not mate until they are about 15 years old and most females will give birth to a single calf about every four years. This 'baby' will weigh about 100kg and be almost one metre tall at birth. Although the calf will eat vegetation food after a few months, it will continue to nurse on its mother's milk until it is at least two years old.

Q —

Do giant squid really exist and how big are they?

A —

Architeuthis, the giant squid, is the largest known animal never to have been observed in its natural habitat. Different species have been washed ashore, dead or dying, over the years and they have been found in commercial fishing nets and the stomachs of sperm whales. However, because they live in extremely deep waters, giant squid remain elusive. We do know that they are the largest invertebrates on Earth, reaching up to 20 metres in length. They also have the largest eyes of any animal ever known, some 40 centimetres in diameter.

Q —

What do swans eat?

A —

Mute swans, which are common in Ireland, eat mostly water plants and insects.

Q —

My shoes are over a year old and still squeak – it is like having squirrels on my feet. Do squirrels squeak?

A —

Squirrels can be very noisy rodents. In their repertoire of noises they can produce chattering, barking, growling and – yes, squeaking.

Q —

What do you call a group of pheasants?

A —

A nide.

Q —

What do you call a group of kangaroos?

A —

A mob (but don't let them hear you).

Ray, why do dogs chase cars? It's not like they're going to catch one and eat it!— *Rachel, Corcaigh*

Good question, and here's a good answer from TV3 vet Pete Wedderburn.

A —

As far as dogs are concerned every time they chase a car they win because the car always runs away so for dogs it's a win win situation and they learn that cars are great things to chase because they don't turn around and shout at them or turn around and bite them, they run away every time. And that's why dogs love it so much!

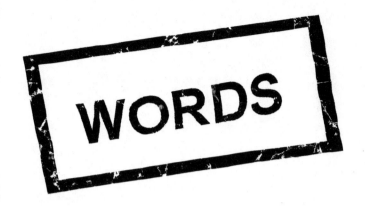

If quizzes are quizzical, what are tests?
— *Anal Anthony*

What happens if you're scared half to death twice?
— *Lisa*

What mean sod put an 's' in lisp?
— *Martin, Cork*

Q —

Where does the saying 'the hair of the dog' originate from – in relation to a hangover cure?

A —

Some ancient civilisations believed that a cure for rabies, and other diseases contracted from a dog bite, was to place a hair from the dog that bit you into the wound. Today 'the hair of the dog' refers to the belief that you can cure a morning hangover by having another drink of whatever you were drinking the night before!

Q —

I say that the phrase 'caught between the devil and the deep blue sea' is a nautical term pertaining to the repair of timber. Am I right?

A —

There is some debate as to the exact origin of this phrase but it is believed to relate to seams on ships, which were particularly difficult to caulk and were known as 'devil seams'. (Caulking was the practice of driving oakum, old rope fibres, between the planks and then covering the seam with hot tar, rendering it waterproof.) The most difficult seams to caulk were those just at, or below the waterline. While the ship was underway unfortunate sailors would be dangled upside down by a rope to carry out this work. As the ship rolled they would often be caught by large waves; occasionally this could lead to the loss of some work tool, which would result in punishment for the luckless sailor. Hence, being caught between the devil seams and the deep blue sea was something to be avoided.

Q —

What does radar stand for?

A —

The name is an acronym formed from RAdio Detection And Ranging. Radar uses reflected radio waves to detect, locate and track distant objects.

Q —

Ray, how many letters in the Irish alphabet?

Eighteen. Irish does not use J, K, Q, V, W, X, Y or Z.

Q —

What does the GI stand for in GI Jane?

A —

In the 1800s the American army began to mark its supplies with the initials 'GI' for 'Government Issue'. These initials soon came to be associated with anything connected to the army, even the personnel. Thus an American soldier is now known simply as a GI.

Q —

Where did the expression 'couldn't swing a cat' come from?

A —

This well-known phrase has nothing to do with domestic felines. The 'cat' in question is the notorious cat-o'-nine-tails, a particularly vicious whip made with nine thin strips of leather, which was used to punish sailors on sailing ships. Such

53

whippings would have to take place up on deck because the ceilings below deck were so low that it was impossible to swing a cat-o'-nine-tails!

Q —

Why are piggy banks so called?

A —

In old English the word 'pygg' referred to a type of orange clay with which people made all kinds of useful objects, including dishes and jars to hold small coins. The first piggy banks appeared in Western Europe between 1500 and 1700. It is possible that somebody asked a potter to make a pygg jar and the potter mistakenly shaped the vessel like a pig, giving us the very first piggy bank.

Q —

Where does the word 'culchie' come from?

A —

The origin of the word 'culchie', meaning a farmworker, is uncertain but it may have been derived from the first syllable of Kiltimagh, Co. Mayo.

Q —

Why are English people called limeys?

A —

The term dates from the late nineteenth century when sailors in the British Navy were made to drink lime juice to prevent scurvy (a disease then common in sailors and caused by vitamin C deficiency).

Q —

What do the initials SAS stand for?

A —

The Special Air Service (SAS) dates from World War II when it was created as a desert raiding force to weaken Rommel's logistics network in North Africa.

Q —

Why is it that when you feel unwell you are 'below par' but when you are doing well at golf you are also 'below par'?

A —

Par means an average level or standard considered to be normal. It comes from the Latin meaning 'equal'. Unlike most sports, where the object is to achieve a higher score than your opponent, in golf the idea is to complete a round in the lowast possible number of strokes. So to be 'below par' in golf terms, means to be better than the average, whereas when it comes to your health, being 'below par' means you're less than average.

Q —

Ray, you know the saying or exclamation 'Gordon Bennett!! – well, who was Gordon Bennett?

A —

It is widely believed that this expression comes from the popularity and infamy of James Gordon-Bennett Jr. His father, a Scotsman, emigrated to the US and founded the New York Herald in 1835. James Jr. was born in 1841 into a very privileged life. As a young man he lived as a playboy, gaining a degree of notoriety for his extravagance. At a New Year's Eve party in 1877, at a party hosted by his prospective in-laws, he got so drunk that he proceeded to urinate into a fireplace before the assembled revellers. However, he was also known for his philanthropy and his willingness to finance scientific expeditions. He funded Stanley's trip to Africa in search of Dr Livingstone and an ill-fated expedition to the North Pole. Today there are islands in Siberia named after him. He was also a patron of sport, establishing yachting, balloon, aeroplane and motor races, some of which still bear his name. His flamboyant and sometimes outrageous antics are believed to have been the inspiration for the exclamation 'Gordon Bennett!'.

Q —

Where does the phrase 'Achilles' heel' come from?

A —

The term refers to a small but potentially fatal weakness. In Homer's *Iliad* (the story of the Trojan War) the Greek hero Achilles is made invulnerable by being immersed in the river Styx as a baby. Unfortunately, his mother forgets to dip in the heel by which she is holding him and this becomes his only weak spot. He is eventually fatally wounded in the heel by an arrow fired by Paris.

Q —

Why is it called a 'dashboard' when it only goes at the same speed as the rest of the car?

A —

The dashboard was originally the mudguard on a horse-drawn carriage and the word was adopted to apply to the panel in front of the earliest car drivers. The term 'dash' used to carry the meaning 'to splash or spatter' but this is now obsolete.

Q —

Which was named first, the fruit or the colour orange?

A —

The fruit was named first, the English word 'orange' coming from old French and, much further back, from the ancient Sanskrit word 'naraga'. Orange, not being a primary colour but a mixture of red and yellow, would certainly have been named after the fruit whose skin it resembles.

Q —

What's the beast that is half man, half horse called?

A —

A centaur. It is a creature from Greek mythology with a dodgy reputation. As followers of the wine god, Dionysus, centaurs were notorious for their drunkenness and for their habit of kidnapping hapless maidens. The one exception to this stereotype was the noble centaur Chiron, a teacher to the Greek heroes Jason and Achilles.

Q —

What is a mnemonic?

A —

It is a memory aid or a method to improve the memory. The best known mnemonic is probably the one designed to recall the colours of the rainbow: Richard of York Gained Battles In Vain'. The first letter of each word represents a colour: red, orange, yellow, green, blue, indigo, violet. The alternative version, for those not interested in history, is: Ran Out Yesterday, Got Blotto In Vineyard.

Q —

Why are potatoes called spuds in Ireland?

A —

The word 'spud' doesn't actually have Irish origins. It comes from New Zealand and first appeared in print around 1845 in E. J. Wakefield's *Adventure in New Zealand*, apparently in a discussion of local slang: 'Pigs and potatoes were respectively represented by "grunters" and "spuds."' The experts' best guess about the origin of 'spud' traces it to a type of short-handled gardening spade also known since about 1667 as a 'spud', used for digging up, you guessed it, potatoes. It may be that the use of 'spuddy' (one who digs with a spud) as a slang term for a potato seller led to the vegetable itself coming to be known as a spud, but at least some connection between the tool name and the vegetable name seems certain.

Q —

What exactly is a 'curate's egg'?

A —

The phrase 'curate's egg' refers to something which is not completely satisfactory, something which has both good and bad points. It comes from a cartoon which featured in the British satirical magazine

Punch in November 1895. The cartoon showed a timid curate eating breakfast with his bishop. The bishop says, 'I'm afraid you've got a bad egg, Mr Jones,' to which the curate, not wishing to give offence, replies, 'Oh no, my Lord, I assure you that parts of it are excellent!'

What is the difference between flammable and inflammable?

Good question. It would be reasonable to suppose that one is the opposite of the other. Not so. Flammable and inflammable mean exactly the same thing, i.e. easily set on fire or easily excited.

Where does the phrase 'to lynch someone' come from?

To lynch someone means to summarily punish without a legal trial. The term is believed to refer to the antics of Captain William Lynch, a planter and justice of the peace in Virginia, USA. During the American Revolution he presided over a vigilante tribunal and the earliest recorded use of the term 'to lynch', in 1811, refers to him.

Q —

What does Aer Lingus mean?

A —

Aer Lingus Teoranta was registered as a private airline company by the Irish government in April 1936. The name is an anglicisation of the Irish phrase 'aer loingeas', meaning 'air fleet'.

Q —

Where did the word cobweb come from?

A —

Cob comes from an old English word, 'coppe', meaning 'spider'. Web simply means woven fabric.

Q —

Why is the US dollar called a buck?

It is a shortening of buckskin, which was used as a unit of exchange in times of barter on the American frontier.

Q —

Where does the term 'cold turkey' come from?

A —

The term refers to the state of drug withdrawal, particularly from heroin. In drug withdrawal the addict's blood is pumped by the heart to the major internal organs, leaving the skin white and with goose bumps, i.e. like turkey skin.

Q —

When people say 'let's start from scratch', what is causing the itch?

A —

This term has been around from the middle of the 18th century and was originally a sporting term. The 'scratch' was a line drawn on the ground.

In the case of racing it was the starting line but it also applied to bare-knuckle boxing, in which case it was the line drawn across the ring to which the boxers were brought to begin the bout. In cricket it indicated the crease, the line drawn in front of the stumps where the batsman stands. In a race where handicaps were applied the people starting from the line had no advantage and so were 'starting from scratch'.

Q —

What is a zephyr?

A —

The term usually applies to a gentle, warming breeze. It can also mean a thin, gauzy fabric of the type worn by athletes.

Q —

What exactly does 'to pull the wool over your eyes' mean?

A —

If you pull the wool over somebody's eyes you are deceiving them. The phrase dates from 19th century America, in the days when wealthy men wore powdered wigs. The word 'wool' refers to the wig. To pull the wool over a man's eyes was to temporarily blind him.

Q —

Why are foolscap pages so called?

A —

Foolscap paper was commonly used in offices before the introduction of the now familiar A4, A5, etc. It was named for the watermark of a fool's cap (jester's hat with bells) which it carried.

Q —

Where did the saying 'take a raincheck' come from?

A —

This is another American phrase which has become common parlance on this side of the Atlantic. A raincheck was originally a voucher issued when a baseball game was rained off. It would allow the spectator to view a future game free of charge. The term spread to other types of sporting events and eventually came to mean any offer that is not taken up immediately.

Q

I've asked English majors but no one seems to know the origin of OK – do you?

A —

There are many theories on the origins of OK (or okay) but the most plausible is that the letters stand for 'orl korrect', a phonetic spelling of 'all correct' used facetiously in early 19th century America. By a happy coincidence the letters OK were also the initials of Old Kinderhook, US President Martin Van Buren (a native of Kinderhook, New York State), and were used in his campaign slogan for the election of 1840 – about the same time as the first recorded use of OK in print.

Q —

Where does the saying 'Hobson's choice' come from?

A —

Tobias Hobson (1544–1631) was immortalised by Milton. He was a Cambridge stable manager who hired out horses. He insisted that customers take the horse of his choosing or none at all. Thus, Hobson's choice is no choice at all.

Q —

What is Murphy's Law?

A —

Firstly, Murphy's Law is not 'anything that can go wrong will'. This is Finagle's Law of Dynamic Negatives, popularised by science fiction writer Larry Niven. Murphy's Law states that, 'If there are two or more ways to do something, and one of those ways can result in a catastrophe, then someone will do it'.

Edward A. Murphy Jr. was an engineer on a series of 1949 US Air Force experiments to test human tolerance to acceleration. One experiment involved a set of sixteen accelerometers fixed to different parts of a subject's body. There were two ways in which each sensor could be glued to its mount. (You're ahead of me now, aren't you?)

Naturally, someone managed to install all sixteen the wrong way around. As a result of this episode Murphy constructed his famous law, which was quoted at a press conference a few days later by the test subject, Major John Paul Stapp. The truth of Murphy's Law struck a chord with many and it quickly became popular in aerospace engineering and other technical disciplines. It first appeared in *Webster's Dictionary* in 1958.

Q —

Where did the word 'codswallop' come from?

A —

At the end of the nineteenth century 'wallop' was a popular slang term for beer. When Hiram Codd developed a new soft drink in a novelty bottle it was widely disparaged by beer drinkers and the term 'codswallop', meaning a load of rubbish, was born.

Q —

Where did the term 'the third degree' originate?

A —

You may find it hard to believe if you've watched too many cops and robbers films, but the term actually comes from Freemasonry. The Third Degree is the highest rank in Freemasonry, to which someone is only admitted after exhaustive examination of his qualifications and fitness to hold the office.

Q —

What do the letters JCB stand for on construction machinery?

A —

They are the initials of the company's founder, Joseph Cyril Bamford, who started JCB in Uttoxeter, England in 1945. Today, JCB excavators and loaders are seen on building sites the world over. More than seventy percent of JCB's production is exported to 140 countries. Joseph Cyril died in 2001 but the JCB company is still privately owned by the Bamford family.

Q —

Why is a midwife called a midwife?

A —

'Mid' is probably from the old English meaning 'with'. Therefore the midwife was somebody who stayed 'with the wife' during her confinement and assisted at the birth of the baby. This explains why midwife is not a feminine noun – it refers to both male and female maternity nurses.

Q —

Where did the phrase 'Bob's your uncle' come from?

A —

'Bob's your uncle', meaning that all is well, owes its origins to British Prime Minister Lord Salisbury, whose first name was Robert. During his premiership, in the late 1880s, his nephew A.J. Balfour received rapid promotion through the cabinet and became Secretary of State for Ireland. Uncle Bob saw to it that all was well for his nephew.

Q —

Why is a baker's dozen 13?

A —

There are two major theories as to the origin of the baker's dozen. It is certainly several centuries old. In times when bread was the staple diet of most of the population it was illegal to sell underweight loaves and heavy penalties could be incurred for this offence. It became a common practice for bakers to give their customers an extra loaf on every dozen so that they were sure of meeting the minimum weight standards laid down by law.

The second theory relates to a 16th century English law which allowed hucksters (wholesalers or middlemen) to purchase 13 units for the price of a dozen. This was their profit margin. So if you purchased a baker's dozen you were getting the wholesale price.

Q —

Where does the term 'blue blood' come from?

A —

This is a direct translation from the Spanish phrase 'sangre azul'. When the north African Moors controlled Castile, the Spanish nobility living there liked to distance themselves by claiming that they were pure bred. They would point to their veins, which appeared bluer in colour than those of the dark-skinned Moors. Although this was simply because the veins showed up more clearly under their lighter skin, the Castilians took it to be a mark of their superior breeding and the term 'blue blood' came to refer to those of aristocratic birth. The phrase was adopted into the English language in the 1830s.

Q —

Does the name Kennedy mean 'ugly head' in Irish?

A —

There are three schools of thought on this one. The first relates to the tree helmets in the traditional Kennedy coat of arms and the Irish 'O'Cinneide', which is interpreted as 'helmet-headed'. The second is that the name comes from the Irish 'cineadh', meaning 'nation'. However in Scotland, where another, distinct Kennedy family evolved, the interpretation of the Gaelic name is indeed accepted to be 'ugly-headed'!

Q —

What is the origin of the word 'deadline' – is it as ominous as it sounds?

During the American Civil War it was often hard to contain the large numbers of prisoners taken. A line would be marked in the ground to form a corral and armed sentries would be posted around it. Any prisoner attempting escape by crossing the line would be shot dead.

Q —

Where does the term 'white elephant' come from?

A —

A white elephant is a possession whose upkeep is a financial burden. The saying is believed to derive from the practice of a particular King of Siam of giving a white elephant as a gift to troublesome courtiers. The very rare and expensive gift would have to be kept by the recipient but the cost of its upkeep would be ruinous.

Q —

Where does the phrase 'to give the cold shoulder' come from?

A —

This goes back to mediaeval times and the days of knights errant. When an adventuring knight stopped at an inn he would be served a hot meal but the common traveller would be offered cold meat, often a shoulder of mutton. To give someone the cold shoulder eventually came to mean to treat them as if they were unworthy or to be deliberately unfriendly to them.

Q —

Why do people say 'God bless you' when somebody sneezes?

A —

When Gregory the Great became Pope in the 6th century, plague was rife in Europe. Gregory called for unceasing prayer for God's intercession. It became the custom to bless someone when they sneezed as this was believed by many to be an early symptom of plague.

Q —

Why is an Allen key so called?

A —

If you are not into DIY and don't own a bicycle you may not even know what this is! An Allen key is an L-shaped implement, somewhere between a key and a screwdriver and it is used to tighten and loosen Allen screws, which have a hexagonal recess in the head. It is named after the Allen Manufacturing Company of Hartford, Connecticut, USA.

Q —

An umbrella used to be called a gamp – why?

A —

Although rarely used today, the term 'gamp' for an umbrella was once very common. It comes from the Charles Dickens novel *Martin Chuzzlewit*, in which the character Sarah Gamp always carries an umbrella.

Q —

Why do people shout 'mayday' when disaster is imminent?

A —

This is the internationally recognised communications distress call, used especially by ships and aircraft. It comes directly from the French 'm'aider', meaning 'help me'.

Q —

What does 'carpe diem' mean?

A —

This Latin phrase is usually translated as 'seize the day', i.e. live life to the full. A more correct interpretation is 'pluck the day' as one would pick a piece of ripe fruit. The sentiment remains the same!

Q —

Is it true that golf stands for 'gentlemen only, ladies forbidden'?

A —

Whilst it is easy to see how this myth developed, the word golf is not an acronym. It was recorded as long ago as 1457 when the Scottish Parliament banned the sport because it was interfering with archery practice. The word probably derives from the old Dutch or German word 'kolb', meaning a club.

Q —

What is the most common surname in Ireland?

A —

Would you believe – Murphy?

Q —

Where does the expression 'keeping up with the Joneses' come from?

A —

This was the title of a strip cartoon which ran in the *New York Globe* and other newspapers for several years. It first appeared in 1913. The cartoonist, Arthur Momand, used the Joneses and their neighbours to illustrate the nature of social rivalry.

Q —

Why is the Green Room so called?

A —

The Green Room is where actors can relax before and after a performance. There are a multitude of theories as to why it is called the Green Room. The term has been in common use since the 17th century. It may have originated in Shakespearean times when actors waiting to perform in the Globe Theatre waited outside, under the trees or 'in the green'. Actors can be very superstitious so you will never find a green Green Room as to paint it this colour is considered unlucky!

Q —

What exactly does 'to paint the town red' mean?

A —

The term today means to have a great night out, but it has gruesome origins. When the Roman Empire was expanding, its soldiers got into the habit of painting the walls of a newly-conquered town with the blood of the inhabitants. As this was a celebration of their victory the activity was accompanied by drinking and festivity.

Q —

What does the 'D' in D–Day stand for?

A —

D–Day is often thought to refer to Operation Overlord, the invasion of Normandy by Allied forces on 6th June 1944 and a major turning point in World War II. However, it is a common military term which means 'the day of the operation'. It is used when the actual date is not fixed or is not common knowledge. The 'D' stands for day and is only for emphasis (instead of saying 'The day'). By the same token the exact time at which an operation is to commence is known as H–hour.

Q —

Where did the phrase 'a cock and bull story' come from?

A —

It means a fanciful or incredible story and may have originated from one of two sources. It might be nothing more spectacular than a reference to the fables and tales of old where animals were supposed to speak. Or it may have originated in

Stony, Stratford in Buckinghamshire, England.

This was where coaches travelling between London and Birmingham would stop to change horses at one of the village's two pubs, one called The Cock and the other The Bull. Exaggerated stories exchanged between groups of travellers from England's two major centres of population may have given rise to the expression.

Q —

Where did the expression 'mad as a hatter' come from?

A —

In times past mercury was widely used in the making of hats. Mercury is highly toxic and can have a number of effects on the nervous system. Some of the results of mercury poisoning are excitability, loss of coordination, tremors and dementia. As hatters (the makers and sellers of hats) commonly exhibited these symptoms they were often labelled as mad.

Q —

What colour exactly is khaki and where does the word come from?

A —

Khaki is a dull brownish-yellow. The word can also refer to the tough cotton cloth used for military uniforms. It comes from the Urdu word 'akí', meaning 'dust-coloured'.

Q —

What do the letters RSVP stand for on an invitation?

A —

'Respondez s'il vous plait' (that's French for 'please reply'!).

Q —

What is the meaning of 'kamikaze'?

A —

The word today is generally used to describe very reckless or self-destructive behaviour. Its origin goes back to World War II when Japanese suicide pilots flew aircraft packed with explosives into enemy targets. The world 'kamikaze' literally means 'divine wind'.

Q —

Where does the expression 'pig iron' come from and what exactly is it?

A —

Pig iron is crude iron from a smelting furnace, roughly shaped for storage or transportation. The smelted iron runs into a channel called a sow, the lateral branches of which are called pigs. This is where the iron cools and becomes pig iron. It can be further processed to make steel and other alloys.

Q —

When you listen in on a conversation are you eavesdropping or earsdropping?

A —

To eavesdrop is to deliberately listen to a conversation not intended for your ears. The word goes back to the days when most houses did not have the luxury of gutters. Rain dripped from the roof but this was projected well beyond the walls of the house. The dry area between the wall and the dripping rain was known as the eavesdrip and later as the eavesdrop. If you took shelter here you would receive some protection from the elements but you could also overhear what was being said inside the house.

Q —

Where does the phrase 'to get the sack' come from?

A —

This dates back to the days when tradesmen owned all their own tools and would carry them from job to job in a bag or sack. If someone was dismissed they would leave the job with their sack.

Q —

Please tell me that 'cul de sac' is French – my friend thinks it is Irish!

A —

The phrase 'cul de sac' is indeed French and its literal meaning is 'bottom of the bag', meaning anything that is closed at one end. When used on street signs it means a dead-end.

Q —

Where does the expression 'the apple of your eye' come from?

A —

This phrase, meaning a cherished person or object, is believed to originate from old English, in which the pupil of the eye was known as the 'apple' of the eye. As the centre of the eye is priceless, it came to serve as a symbol for something cherished.

Q —

Where does the expression 'doolally' come from?

A —

The expression has been shortened from 'doolally tap'. Its origins lie with the British rule of India. In the late nineteenth century the British army had a sanatorium at Deolali, about 160 kilometres north-east of Bombay. Apart from its convalescent function, it also served as a transit camp for soldiers returning to Britain. Soldiers sometimes had to wait several months for a ship to take them home and had no drill or duties to perform at Deolali. Many soldiers embarked on foolish behaviour to relieve the boredom of the camp, some contracting venereal disease and ending up in hospital, others serving gaol terms for their misdeamours. The word 'tap' is Urdu for 'malarial fever'. Thus 'having the doolally tap' meant that a person was exhibiting strange or eccentric behaviour, what we would today call 'cabin fever'.

Q —

Where does the word 'bloke' come from?

A —

It is the word for 'man' in Shelta, the language of the Romany people of Britain and Ireland.

Q —

Where does the word 'anorak' come from?

A —

The word 'anorak', meaning a thick, waterproof, hooded jacket, comes from the Inuit word 'annoraaq'. (Inuit is a language used by Eskimos.)

An 'anorak' is today used colloquially to mean someone who appears to have an over-zealous interest in a certain subject. This term referred originally to the fans of pirate radio station *Radio Caroline*, which was based at sea. To complete a pilgrimage to the station the fans had to take a boat and because the journey was cold and wet they wore anoraks!

FILM & TV

Why is the winner of Miss Universe always from earth?
— *Confused, Athlone*

Why don't the people of Cabot Cove just ask Jessica Fletcher to leave town?

Q —

Ray, what was Morse's first name in the TV series?

A —

Believe it or not, Inspector Morse's first name is Endeavour. This was first revealed in the episode 'Death is now my neighbour'.

Q —

Could you please tell me who were the other characters in *Charlie Brown*?

A —

The entire Peanuts gang are: Charlie Brown, the worrier; Lucy Van Pelt, know-it-all; Linus Van Pelt, blanket boy; Rerun Van Pelt, helmet boy; Snoopy, Charlie Brown's beagle dog; Woodstock, little yellow bird; Franklin, Charlie Brown's friend; Sally, Charlie Brown's younger sister; Peppermint Patty, the Tomboy who calls Charlie Brown 'Chuck'; Shroeder, the piano player; Pig Pen, the really dirty one; Marcie, the smart one.

Q —

Why is a soap opera so called?

A —

A 'soap' is a radio or television serial featuring stock characters in melodramatic domestic situations. The term originated in America in the mid-1930s. The first such commercial radio shows targeted housewives and the sponsors tended to be manufacturers of soap and detergents.

Q —

Hi Ray, I know six names of the Walton children from the TV series but I'm missing the 7th – help me.

A —

John and Olivia Walton's seven children were: John Boy, Jason, Mary Ellen, Ben, Erin, Jim Bob and Elizabeth.

Q —

Am I the only person on the planet who doesn't know who or what the Goons were?

A —

The Goon Show was first broadcast by BBC radio in May 1951 under the title *Crazy People*. Its stars were Spike Milligan, Peter Sellers, Harry Seacombe and Michael Bentine. The name changed and Michael Bentine left after creative differences with Milligan. The name 'Goon' came from a strange being in the Popeye cartoons, which were a favourite of Milligan. *The Goon Show* ran for nine years with 26 shows being broadcast each year.

Q —

Where exactly is Craggy Island?

A —

Craggy Island is in fact Inisheer, the smallest of the Aran Islands. The house in which Father Ted, Dougal and Mrs Doyle live their eccentric lives can be found just outside Killinaboy in Co. Clare.

Q —

When was the first *Star Trek, The Cage,* shown on television?

A —

The Cage was the original pilot for the *Star Trek* series but was considered too challenging for 1965 audiences. However Gene Roddenberry, creator of *Star Trek*, incorporated *The Cage* into a later two-part episode entitled 'The Menagerie'. This was aired on 17th and 24th November 1966. The original version of *The Cage* was shown by NBC in 2000 and is now available on DVD, to the delight of Trekkies everywhere.

Q —

What did the letters U.N.C.L.E. stand for in *The Man From U.N.C.L.E* ?

A —

The initials stand for United Network Command for Law Enforcement, and agents Solo and Kuryakin could be seen on TV screens throughout the mid–1960s.

Q —

What do the initials M.A.S.H. stand for?

A —

Mobile Army Surgical Hospital.

Q —

In the TV show *CHiPS* what were the bikes that the two policemen used? I think they were Harleys.

A —

CHP is an acronym for the California Highway Patrol. In the NBC series, *CHiPs*, which ran from 1977 to 1983, police officers Jon Baker and Francis 'Ponch' Poncherello cruised the Los Angeles highways on Kawasaki 1000 motorcycles. In 1998 a made-for-TV *CHiPs* reunion movie was broadcast by the Turner Cable Network and the boys were riding high-powered BMW bikes.

Q —

What show did the Simpsons first appear on?

A —

The Simpsons first appeared in 1987 as a series of 30-second spots produced for the Emmy Award winning series *The Tracey Ullman Show*. The first of the half-hour shows was broadcast on 14th January 1990. The series has received the Emmy Award for Outstanding Animated Programme on numerous occasions since 1990. Interestingly, creator Matt Groening named the Simpsons after members of his immediate family, with the exception of Bart – that is an anagram of Brat!

Q —

What's Malcolm's last name in *Malcolm in the Middle*?

A —

The family surname has never been revealed, nor have their ages or school grades!

Q —

What is the theme tune to *China Beach*?

A —

Many people remember this very popular show which ran from 1988 to 1991 and told the story of a group of nurses in Vietnam. The theme music was 'Reflections', a 1968 hit for Diana Ross and the Supremes.

Q —

What colour was Mr Ed, the talking horse, and what type of horse was he?

A —

Mr Ed was a palomino – a golden coloured horse with a white mane and tail.

Q —

Who refused to appear on *This Is Your Life*?

A —

Danny Blanchflower was a professional footballer who played for Aston Villa, Spurs and Northern Ireland. On 7th February 1961, on live TV, Eamon Andrews said, 'Danny Blanchflower, this is your life!' and Danny famously replied, 'Oh no it isn't!'

Q —

Could you tell me when the last *Only Fools And Horses* was made?

A —

First things first! Del and Rodney Trotter originally hit our screens on 8th September 1981 and spent the next 15 years scheming to become millionaires. The last episode, 'Time On Our Hands', was broadcast on 29th December 1996. In it, the Trotters finally achieve their ambition. Del finds an old timepiece which has been in his lock-up for years and it fetches millions when auctioned at Sotheby's. There have been two Christmas specials since 1996: 'If They Could See us Now' and 'Stranger on the Shore' in 2002.

Q —

How many James Bond films did Timothy Dalton star in?

A —

Timothy Dalton was approached in 1969 to play James Bond in *On Her Majesty's Secret Service* but considered himself too young. He was considered for the part again in 1984, when Roger Moore was talking about leaving the role, but his schedule was too busy to accommodate *A View To A Kill*. His first film portrayal of Bond was in *The Living Daylights* in 1987 and this was followed by *Licence To Kill* in 1989.

Q —

Help! Trying to find out whether *The Hunt for Red October*, *Patriot Games* and *Clear and Present Danger* are part of a series of movies.

A —

These films are all based on books from the 'Jack Ryan' series written by Tom Clancy.

Q —

Can you tell me the name of Harpo Marx's autobiography?

A —

Harpo was the silent Marx Brother so what else would his autobiography be called but *Harpo Speaks!*

Q —

Who played Hannibal Lector in the original version of *Red Dragon*, which was called *Manhunter*?

A —

In *Manhunter* the part of Hannibal Lector was played by hard-working Scottish actor Brian Cox.

Q —

Was Michael Jackson in a different *Wizard of Oz*?

A —

Yes. It was called *The Wiz* and was Disney's film version of a Broadway play, in which Oz is transplanted to New York City. Dorothy was played by Diana Ross, Richard Pryor was The Wiz and Michael Jackson was Scarecrow.

Q —

Whatever happened to Condorman?

A —

Disney's Condorman was the world's most unlikely superhero. Comic strip writer and artist

Woody Wilkins won't allow his creation, Condorman, do anything that he can't do himself. The opening scene of the movie shows Woody swooping from the Eiffel Tower in his Condorman outfit. The film starred Michael Crawford, best known as Frank Spencer in *Some Mothers Do 'Ave Them* and as the phantom in the Andrew Lloyd Webber musical *Phantom of the Opera*. The movie *Condorman* disappointed at the box office and was out of circulation for several years. However, a collector's edition was released on DVD and video in 1999, to the delight of fans everywhere.

Q —

Where can I get all nine series of *Seinfeld* on DVD or video?

A —

Famously, *Seinfeld* has never been released on DVD or video – much to the annoyance of fans. There are many websites selling pirate copies but the only legitimate video performance from Jerry Seinfeld is his stand-up 'I'm Telling You For The Last Time'.

Q —

Was Mrs Bartlet from *The West Wing* in the movie *Grease*?

A —

Yes, Stockard Channing played Rizzo (the feisty one) in *Grease*.

Q —

How many spikes of hair do Bart and Lisa Simpson have?

A —

Because they are two dimensional it is difficult to get an accurate number. However, after exhaustive research and many hours of observation we have established that Bart has nine spikes and Lisa has eight.

Q —

What does the acronym ACE stand for after people's names in film credits?

A —

The society of American Cinema Editors was founded in 1950. Film editors are voted into membership on the basis of their professional achievements, including their dedication and commitment to excellence in the craft of film editing.

Q —

What crime were the A-Team sent to prison for?

A —

A-Team were a former crack commando unit who fought together during the Vietnam War. Towards the end of the war they were wrongly tried and imprisoned for a bank robbery in Hanoi. They escaped from Fort Bragg maximum security prison and began righting wrongs all over America.

Q —

From which film does the frequently quoted 'Be afraid, be very afraid' come?

A —

This line is uttered by Geena Davis in *The Fly*. She plays the love interest to Jeff Goldblum as the eccentric scientist/fly.

Q —

When Maggie goes through the checkout at the opening of each episode of *The Simpsons* how much registers on the till?

A —

Maggie is shown as costing $847.63, a figure once estimated to be the amount required to keep a baby for one month in the US. (It has never been adjusted for inflation!)

Q —

Why are the American Academy Awards called 'Oscars'?

A —

The most commonly accepted story about the origin of the name Oscar is that Academy libararian (and later executive director) Margaret Herrick said that the statuette resembled her Uncle Oscar. The name was used officially by the Academy for the first time in 1939.

Q —

Where is *Last of the Summer Wine* filmed?

A —

It is filmed in the village of Holmfirth, in the Kirklees district of Yorkshire. Holmfirth is the main town of the Holme Valley and has a long history in film making, the local Bamforth family having been pioneers of motion pictures in the early 1900s. It is possible to take a tour of the Summer Wine locations, including a stop at the Wrinkled Stocking Tea Rooms!

Q —

One thing that often puzzles me is when you look at the credits at the end of a programme or film. What is a 'key grip'?

A —

The key grip is the right-hand man of the cinematographer. It is his job to set up lighting and arrange camera moves to get the exact desired effect. He has to be mechanically inventive and creatively imaginative.

Is it true that Willie O'Dea was used as a model for the game show *Guess Who*?
— *Limerick Listener*

Q —

Is it true that Jim Morrison's grave in Paris is guarded 24 hours a day and has a fire burning there continuously?

A —

Jim Morrison is buried in Père Lachaise Cemetery in Paris, along with many other luminaries including Oscar Wilde. Since its desecration by neo-Nazis some years ago, Morrison's grave has been under a 24-hour police guard. It is visited frequently and candles burn there constantly.

Q —

Did Catherine Zeta Jones ever appear in a film about the *Titanic*?

A —

Yes. *Titanic* was a 1996, made-for-TV film in which Zeta Jones starred with George C. Scott.

Q —

What was John Wayne's real name?

A ▬

John Wayne was born on 26th May 1907 with the name Marion Michael Morrison. It is unlikely that he would have become the archetypal Hollywoood western hero had he kept it!

Q ▬

Is it true that Queen Elizabeth II has two birthdays and if so, why?

A ▬

Queen Elizabeth II was born on 21st April 1926. However, it is customary to celebrate the British sovereign's birthday on a day during the summer. Since 1805 this 'official birthday' has been marked by the Trooping of the Colour, a ceremony which usually takes place on the second Saturday in June.

Q ▬

What is Cher's real name?

A ▬

Cher's real name is . . . Cher! Well, it's a little more exotic in its entirety – Cherilyn Sarkisian LaPierre.

Q —

Ray, where is the great Jimi Hendrix buried?

A —

Jimi Hendrix is buried in Greenwood Memorial Park, Renton, in Washington State. Renton is about half-an-hour's drive from Seattle.

Q —

Why is Billy Connolly called 'The Big Yin'?

A —

In Scotland 'big yin' simply means 'big one'. It is the opposite of 'wee man'. Billy is six feet tall and was reckoned to be a 'big yin' by his shipyard colleagues, long before he became famous.

Q —

Can you tell me where Elvis Costello was born? I think it was Ireland but everyone thinks I am wrong. Please help.

A —

Everyone is right. Elvis Costello was born Declan MacManus in London in 1954. His stage name came from Elvis Presley and his mother's maiden name, Costello.

Q —

How old was Andrew Strong when he made *The Commitments*?

A —

For those too young to remember, *The Commitments* is an Alan Parker film about the birth of a soul band in Dublin (if you've never seen it, rent the video or DVD). Andrew Strong's mature performance and incredible voice belied the fact that he was only nineteen when the film was made.

Q —

Ray, can you settle an argument please? Is Clint Eastwood Charlie Chaplin's son?

A —

Don't know where you heard this one, but the more common urban myth is that Stan Laurel (of

Laurel and Hardy) was Clint's daddy. The truth, however, is that Clinton Eastwood Sr. fathered Clint Eastwood Jnr.

Q —

What age is Mel Gibson?

A —

Mel Gibson was born on 3rd January 1956 in Peekskill, New York. During his childhood, when his older brothers would have been eligible for the Vietnam War draft, the family relocated to Sydney, Australia, his mother's hometown.

Q —

Ray and Jenny, can you please fix it so that my best friend knows that Boy George is from Ireland and not England as she thinks, the eejit! Thanks.

A —

Don't you hate the taste of humble pie? Boy George was born George Alan O'Dowd on 14th June 1961 in Bexleyheath, Kent, England to Irish parents, Dinah and Gerry O'Dowd.

Q —

Whatever happened to Big Daddy, the wrestler?

A —

Big Daddy was born, believe it or not, Shirlie Crabtree in Halifax, West Yorkshire in 1930. He died following a stroke in 1997.

Q —

Is Monica Seles a true American or was she originally from Europe?

A —

Monica Seles was born in Novi Sad, Serbia (Yugoslavia). She now lives in Florida, USA.

Q —

Ray, how old exactly is Raquel Welch?

A —

Jo Raquel Tejada was born on the 5th September 1940 in Chicago.

Q —

Did Sylvester Stallone star in a porn movie before he became famous?

A —

Stallone's first film role was indeed in the porn movie *Party at Kitty and Stud's,* released in 1970. After the success of *Rocky,* the 1976 triple Oscar-winning film which made Stallone a star, the owners of *Party at Kitty and Stud's* re-released it under the new title *The Italian Stallion.*

Q —

Was Morrissey born in Ireland?

A —

Stephen Patrick Morrissey was born on 22nd May 1959 in Manchester, England.

Q —

Is Viggo Mortensen American or Norwegian?

A —

Viggo Mortensen, now known to *Lord of the Rings* fans the world over as Aragorn, is American. He was born in Manhattan, New York on 20th October 1958 to a Danish father and an American mother.

Q —

How old is Kylie?

A —

Kylie Minogue was born on 28th May 1968 in Melbourne, Australia.

Q —

What is Meat Loaf's real name?

A —

Meat Loaf's real name is Marvin Lee Aday.

Q —

Where is Russell Crowe from?

A —

Russell Crowe was born in Auckland, New Zealand on 7th April 1964, of Norwegian and Maori ancestry. When he was four his family moved to Sydney, Australia. He began his acting career at the age of six!

Q —

What age is Leslie Nielsen from *The Naked Gun* films? He has looked about seventy for the past 25 years!

A —

He was born on 11th February 1926.

Q —

Is it true that the late, great Dean Martin has 'Everybody Loves Somebody Sometime' on his headstone?

Yes. The only other writings on his headstone are the dates of his birth and death.

I know Jonathon Ross's mother works on *Eastenders*. Is she an actress or the tea-lady?

Martha Ross has been an extra on *Eastenders* since it first hit the small screen.

Can you tell me if the actress who plays Carrie in *Sex and the City* was in the movie *Footloose*?

Yes. Sarah Jessica Parker played Rusty in the 1984 film, which also starred Kevin Bacon.

Q —

What ever happened to the Karate Kid?

A —

The incredibly young-looking Ralph Macchio is still a working actor. He was 22 when he played 14-year-old Daniel in the first *Karate Kid*. He has worked on the Broadway stage and made numerous films since then, one of the more notable being *My Cousin Vinny*.

Q —

When did Roy Orbison die?

A —

Roy Orbison was born 23rd April 1936 and died 6th December 1988.

Q —

What do the initials JRR stand for in JRR Tolkien, author of *The Lord of The Rings* and is he still alive?

A —

John Ronald Reuel Tolkien died on 2nd September 1973 at the age of 81.

Q —

Are Hugh Grant and Richard E. Grant related?

A —

No, they are not. Grant is actually Richard's middle name; the E. stands for Esterhuysen.

Why is bread square when slices of ham are oval?
— *Frustrated in Donegal*

Please tell us why do someone else's chips
always taste better. Thanks. — *Anon*

How is it that when you put Jaffa Cakes and
Digestives into the same jar, the Jaffa Cakes go
hard and the Digestives go soft? — *Mairead*

Q —

How does alcohol make you drunk?

A —

Alcohol is a general depressant. It inhibits receptors in the central nervous system, making it difficult to control your own body! It has a similar effect to an anaesthetic, just not as severe.

Q —

When you are nervous about something and you go for a drink beforehand, why is it called Dutch courage?

A —

In the seventeenth century the Dutch captain of a man-o-war called *The Hollander* began the practice of opening a hogshead of brandy on deck before going into battle and telling his sailors to help themselves. A hogshead is an extremely large cask, so there would have been no shortage of Dutch courage aboard *The Hollander*!

Q —

Why is there a worm in a tequila bottle?

A —

It is a popular misconception that there is a worm in every bottle of tequila. In fact, the worm (which is not even a worm but a butterfly larva!) is found only in genuine mescal, a type of tequila distilled from the agave plant. As the larva inhabits only the agave plant its inclusion signifies genuine mescal made in the traditional way. The tradition of placing the larva in the mescal is believed to have been initiated by Aztec priests to instil a life spirit into the drink. Many of today's mescal drinkers prize the 'worm' as an aphrodisiac!

Q —

Why can't you eat turkey eggs?

A —

No reason – they are perfectly edible. However, the main reason that turkey eggs are not mass marketed is because of their size. In particular they would not be compatible with the requirements of cookery books. A large chicken egg weighs about 50 grams while a turkey egg is nearer to 80 grams. This discrepancy could lead to culinary disasters on a major scale!

Q —

What is the difference between raisins, sultanas and currants?

A —

Not a lot – they are all dried grapes. The raisin is a partially dried grape, the sultana is a seedless raisin and the currant is a small, dried, seedless grape.

Q —

Which has more caffeine – tea or coffee?

A —

Tea contains only about half the caffeine of the equivalent volume of fresh coffee.

Q —

What is a Baked Alaska?

A —

Baked Alaska is a core of ice cream on sponge cake encased in meringue. It is kept in the freezer until required and then placed in a very hot oven for just long enough to cook and brown the meringue. This confection was created in 1876 at Delmonico's Restaurant, New York City, in honour of the newly acquired territory of Alaska.

Q —

What exactly is boxty?

A —

Boxty is a traditional Irish potato cake made from raw and cooked, mashed potatoes. Salt, pepper and onion are added for flavour and flour, milk and egg are used to bind the ingredients, which are then fried in the pan or browned on a griddle.

Q —

Why do restaurants call chicken wings 'buffalo wings'?

A —

This is a term which has crossed the Atlantic in recent years. It describes chicken wings cooked in a barbecue or other spicy sauce and served as an appetiser. Apparently they are so called because they were first served in this manner in a restaurant in Buffalo, New York.

Q —

What's the difference between proof and volume on alcohol bottles?

A —

The answer is 'it depends'! In the USA proof is twice the percentage of alcohol by volume. An 80 proof spirit, for example, is 40% by volume. The UK measures are a little more complex – try the following, but only if you are sober! Any given volume of alcohol weighs less than the same volume of water. Alcohol diluted with water gradually approaches the weight of a similar volume of water. When enough water has been added to pure alcohol that the mixture weighs 12/13 as much as a similar volume of water, the mixture is proof spirit. (This must be measured at exactly 51 degrees Fahrenheit.) The alcohol now equates to 48.24% by weight or 57.06% by volume. As the quantity of alcohol varies from that measure, so the liquid is over-proof or under-proof.

Q —

Who invented chewing gum?

A —

The habit of chewing some form of gum goes back many centuries. The ancient Greeks chewed mastic gum, a resin obtained from the bark of the mastic tree. American colonists learned the habit from the Native American Indians who chewed the resin from spruce trees. This became the first commercial chewing gum when it was sold in the eastern US in the early 1800s. From about 1850 sweetened paraffin wax began to overtake spruce gum in popularity. In Mexico, the gum of choice was chicle, extracted from the sap of the chicle (or naseberry) tree. The Mexican general, Santa Anna, was exiled to New York after he was defeated by the Americans in Texas in 1845. He introduced chicle to the inventor Thomas Adams, who began experimenting with it as a substitute for rubber. Adams tried to make toys, masks, rain boots and other products from the chicle but found it unsuitable. The story goes that while sitting in his workshop one day, tired and frustrated by his failed experiments, he popped a piece of surplus stock into his mouth and started chewing. The idea of adding flavouring to the gum occurred to him and shortly after he opened the world's first chewing gum factory.

Q —

How do seedless grapes grow if they have no seeds to replant them?

A —

'Seedless' grapes do contain seeds at some point but a genetic error prevents each seed from forming its hard outer coat. But seeds are not essential for propagation. Most fruits today are grown from cuttings, taken from a vine or branch. This means that new grapevines are essentially clones of the vine from which they were cut.

Q —

Is rosé wine made with black and white grapes?

A —

Rosé wine is made from black grapes without the stalks. The juice is separated from the pulp as soon as it is sufficiently pink. There are many styles of rosé wine but some of the finest are produced from the Grenache grape.

Q —

Why is orange jam called marmalade?

A —

The word marmalade is derived from the Portuguese name for the quince fruit, 'marmelo'. During the Middle Ages this was considered to be the most useful of fruits, forming the basis for a farmer's preserving for winter. Marmalade as we know it today was first made in Scotland in 1790 by Janet Keillor, a Dundee woman who was trying to find a use for bitter Seville oranges. Her recipe was developed by her son James who opened Keillor's factory, still famous today for its jams and marmalades.

Q —

Is chocolate addictive?

A —

There are many chemicals in chocolate which can help trigger pleasurable effects in our bodies. Phenylethylamine causes the brain to release dopamine (the same chemical that peaks during an orgasm – which could explain why some women prefer chocolate to sex!). Another component, theobromine, is a structural relative of caffeine. It has a less stimulating effect but can increase your pulse rate, and withdrawal from theobromine has been shown to cause migraine. Chocolate also contains tryptophan, an essential amino-acid which plays a role in the production of serotonin. Serotonin is another neurotransmitter essential to general well-being and believed to play a vital role in maintaining a relaxed and well-balanced mood. Some women crave chocolate when they are premenstrual, possibly because it contains high levels of magnesium, an element which is usually deficient prior to menstruation.

Much research has been done into chocolate cravings and the general consensus is that there is no one particularly addictive element – it is the whole package that people want. People use chocolate to pamper or console themselves and to celebrate special occasions. There are many cultural, psychological and physiological factors at play in our love affair with chocolate, apart from the fact that it tastes great!

Q —

Who invented crisps?

A —

The crisp as we know it was first produced by

American chef George Crum in 1853. He was working at a restaurant in New York when a customer complained that his 'French fries' were too thick. Crum made a thinner batch but the diner was still not satisfied. The frustrated chef eventually made a batch of fries which were too thin to eat with a fork, hoping to annoy the customer who was in fact delighted! The potato chip or 'crisp' had been invented.

The first cheese and onion flavoured crisp did not appear until the 1950s when Joe 'Spud' Murphy tired of plain crisps with salt, the only type available until then. He launched his own company, Tayto, in Dublin in 1954 and it is today one of Ireland's leading brand names.

Q —

Why does boiled milk get that annoying skin on top?

A —

The skin is the result of evaporation at the surface of the milk which concentrates proteins there. It is actually a complex of casein and calcium. Skin formation can be minimised by slowing down the rate of evaporation, either by covering the pan or by whipping up a little foam.

Q —

What drink is made from pears?

A —

Perry is a drink made by the same process as cider but with pears instead of apples.

Q —

What nutritional value do mushrooms have?

A —

Mushrooms are a surprisingly nutritious food source. They are high in fibre, low in fat and relatively high in protein. They are high in several of the B vitamins and also biotin and vitamin C. Mushrooms produce maximum nutritional benefit after cooking.

Q —

What was the staple diet in Ireland before the introduction of the potato?

A —

The answer is oats, which grow well in our moist climate, especially in the fertile soil of Leinster. Potatoes became the staple diet when farmers realised that only a small piece of land was required to produce enough spuds to feed a family. The rest of their land could be devoted to oats, which were sold to pay rent.

Q —

Where did the idea of making tea come from?

A —

Legend has it that the origins of tea-making go back over 5,000 years to China. The emperor was touring his realm and stopped to rest one day. His servants were boiling water for the royal party to drink when some dried leaves fell from a nearby bush into the pot. The emperor, something of a scientist, was intrigued by the resulting brown liquid and decided to drink some. He found it refreshing and tea drinking was born.

Q —

Why do dandelions have the reputation for making you wet the bed?

A —

Although we consider the dandelion to be a weed it has a number of culinary and medicinal uses. Young leaves can be eaten raw in a salad; older leaves can be made into soup. The blossoms of the dandelion can be used to make wine. The plant is high in vitamins A and C and is also known for its diuretic effects, i.e. it increases the flow of urine from the body. Other common diuretics include caffeine and alcohol. In France the dandelion is called 'pissenlit', which means 'wet the bed'.

Q —

Are there many calories in a pint of Guinness?

A —

There are 204 calories per draft pint of Guinness. For comparison, a slice of apple pie contains about 405 calories, a banana has 105 and a bottle of regular beer has about 150. Take your pick!

Q —

Do you remember the advert 'melt in your mouth, not in your hand'? Was it Maltesers or M&Ms?

A —

Neither! It was Treats.

Q —

Why does eating chillies or spicy food make you sweat?

A —

Chillies contain capsaicin, which is an irritant – hence the burning sensation and sweating. Pure capsaicin (or 8-methyl-n-vanillyl-6-nonenamide) is a whitish powder which is soluble in alcohol but insoluble in cold water. This is why drinking glass after glass of water won't alleviate the burning effect of a chilli overdose! Unlike other spicy substances like mustard oil, black pepper or ginger, capsaicin produces long-lasting, selective desensitisation by repeated doses of low concentration. In other words, the more chilli you eat the more your tolerance to it will increase.

Q —

Here's one for you Ray. What's the difference between pork, ham and bacon. It's all pig, isn't it?
— *Gerry, Galway*

Kierans Brothers in Drogheda are a well known traditional pork and bacon butchers. We asked them to tell us the difference.

A —

It's one of the most common questions we get asked by our customers and it's a very understandable one. We find that most people can't differentiate between them but there is obviously a difference. And that is that pork is unsalted whereas bacon is salted. In order to turn pork into bacon the pork itself gets cured. And the curing process involves injecting a brine (salt and water) solution into the pork – and that turns it into bacon. And the difference between bacon and ham? Ham is the name given to the hind leg of bacon.

Q —

Ray, the Elephant and Castle in Temple Bar, Dublin is famous for its chicken wings. How do they make them? There have been many imitators but there's no place that does them like the E and C. Any chance you could find out?
— *Starvin Marvin, Dunshaughlin*

Marvin, the bad news is that Elephant and Castle treat their recipe like a state secret. The Chicken wings have been on the menu since December 1989. It is their most popular dish and people have been going to E and C for years solely for the wings. While we couldn't get the recipe from the chef, we did get some people calling the show telling us that they'd figured it out. Here's one recipe and method which was offered by a female caller. We've tried it out and it's pretty close to the famous Elephant and Castle taste.

CHICKEN WINGS

Get a pack and a half of the chicken wings from your butcher or supermarket. Remove the wing tip, leaving the little V joint. Cut that in half again so you have a mini drumstick and a slightly smaller piece. Deep fry your chicken wings for about 6 to 8 minutes, just until they're really crispy and the juices are completely clear.

In the meantime melt about 4 oz of butter add in 2 tablespoons of cider vinegar and 4 to 6 tablespoons of Tabasco sauce. Mix all that together. When the wings are done, toss them in this butter mixture then drain them. Serve them as quickly as possible with a blue cheese dip. To make a blue cheese dip, mix the following ingredients together.

>Half cup of sour cream
>Three quarters of a cup of mayonnaise
>Half a cup of blue cheese crumbled
>1 clove of garlic, crushed
>1 teaspoon of lemon juice
>1 tablespoon of cider vinegar
>2 tablespoons of chopped fresh parsley

Enjoy!

HISTORY

Has anyone ever seen Anthony Worrall Thompson and Henry VIII in the same room . . . I know the latter is dead but you know what I mean!
— *Hugh, Kildare*

Q —

What does GUBU mean? Charlie Haughey used the word.

A —

In 1982 it was discovered that Malcom McArthur, a man sought by the Gardaí in connection with a murder, was living at the home of the Attorney General. Mr Haughey described the situation as 'grotesque, unbelievable, bizarre, unprecedented'. Conor Cruise O'Brien was quick to coin the acronym 'GUBU'.

Q —

I was watching the film *Michael Collins* over Christmas and I got thinking, what ever happened to Kitty Kiernan? Did she ever marry?

A —

Kitty met Michael Collins and Harry Boland in 1917. She and Collins corresponded while he was in London for the Treaty negotiations. Collins was assassinated at Beal na Bláth on 22nd August 1922. Kitty married Felix Cronin in 1925. She died in 1945 and is buried in Glasnevin Cemetery.

Q —

What was Watergate?

A —

Watergate refers to the political scandal in America in the early 1970s which led to the downfall of Republican President Richard Nixon. The name is that of the Watergate Hotel in Washington DC. It was here that the offices of the Democratic National Committee were burgled on 17th June 1972. The burglary, and more importantly the attempted cover-up which followed, eventually led to the impeachment and resignation of Nixon on 8th August 1974.

Q —

Why are clocks put forward one hour in the spring and back in the autumn?

A —

'Daylight saving' was adopted by many European countries and the US during World War I in an effort to conserve fuel by reducing the demand for electricity in the evenings. However, the idea had been put forward as early as 1784 by Benjamin

Franklin, purely as a way of making people more productive. In the European Union, Summer Time begins on the last Sunday in March and ends on the last Sunday in October.

Q —

What are 'glasnost' and 'perestroika'?

A —

These were policies initiated by Mikhail Gorbachov in the USSR during the late 1980s. Glasnost encouraged openness and accountability from government agencies and more disclosure of information. Perestroika was the political and economic restructuring of the USSR, including decentralisation of control over industry and agriculture and some privatisation.

Q —

How did they fill the Royal Canal?

A —

The Royal Canal, running from Dublin to the Shannon, Co. Roscommon, was completed in 1817 at a total cost of £1,421,954 (€1,805,509). The main water supply is from Lough Owel, near Mullingar in Co. Westmeath. This feeds the highest point of the canal, which then descends in both directions, east to Dublin and west to the Shannon.

Q

What do the 12 stars on the European Union flag represent?

A —

The Council of Europe adopted this flag in 1986. The 12 stars were never meant to represent individual countries. The flag's background is a blue sky on which there are 12 gold stars, symbolising perfection and unity.

Q —

In the Northern Ireland legislature, what do the initials MLA stand for?

A

Member of the Legislative Assembly.

Q —

We've lived through the Sixties, Seventies, Eighties and Nineties. What are we in now?

A —

Could it be the Naughties?

Q —

What is the G8?

A —

The G8 is an informal forum which discusses global economic issues at an annual meeting. The countries who participate are France, US, UK, Germany, Japan, Italy, Canada and Russia. The European Union also takes part and is represented by the President of the Commission and the leader of the country holding the European Council presidency. The first such meeting was held in Rambouillet, France in 1975, between only six countries. Canada joined in 1976 and Russia in 1997.

Q —

Why are there two Ls on all the euro coins?

A —

They are the signature of the artist who designed the common side of the euro coins. He is a Belgian by the name of Luc Luycx.

Q —

What's the connection between Che Guevara and Galway?

A —

Ernesto 'Che' Guevara was born in Buenos Aires in 1928, the first child of Ernesto Guevara Lynch and Celia de la Serna. His paternal grandmother, Ana Isabel Lynch, was the daughter of Irish immigrants who had left Galway in Famine times. That is to say, his great-grandparents were Irish.

Q —

Who did Strongbow marry?

A —

The first Anglo-Normans landed in Wexford in 1169. In return for the success of their joint mission, Diarmuid promised his daughter Aoife to his chief ally, Strongbow, along with the kingship of Leinster. In 1170, after the conquest of the city of Waterford, Strongbow and Aoife were married in the cathedral there. Waterford was declared a Royal City in 1171.

Q —

Arthur Guinness signed the lease on St. James's Gate Brewery. How long was it for?

A —

On 31st December 1759 the farsighted young Arthur Guinness signed a lease for 9,000 years at an annual rent of £45 (€57).

Q —

Why did Guinness start to publish the *Guinness Book of Records*?

In 1951 while on a shooting party, Sir Hugh Beaver, then managing director of the Guinness Brewery, became involved in an argument over which was the fastest game bird in Europe. He suspected that a book containing the answers to such questions might prove popular. The brothers Norris and Ross McWhirter, who ran a fact-finding agency in London, were commissioned to compile such a book. The first *Guinness Book of Records* was published in August 1955 and was at the top of the bestsellers list by Christmas. With sales of over 94 million copies in 37 languages, the book itself holds a record as the world's biggest-selling copyright book.

Q —

Does a pope have to die before a new pope is elected or can he retire?

Popes can abdicate but it is extremely unusual. In fact, the last entirely voluntary abdication was as far back as 1294 when Celestine V resigned after less than four months in the job and went back to life as a hermit. There is currently no procedure for removing a pope from office should he become permanently incapacitated.

Q —

Ray, why do most watches in catalogues and jewellers' windows have their hands set at ten to two? Is there a reason?
— Jason, Baltinglass

It's a question we've been asked before and to find out the answer we talked to the professionals at Appleby Jewellers.

A —

The answer is surprisingly simple. It's a tradition that dates back to the early 1960s in Japan, when the Japanese went in to the watch business in a serious way. Traditionally the Japanese tends to try and inject humour into their marketing and they reckoned that a watch looked happy when it was at ten minutes to two as it resembled a smiling face. They called ten minutes to two 'Happy Time'. It's a little bit better than twenty to eight. So that's it, a silly answer, but that's the answer!

SCIENCE

If swimming is such good exercise, why are whales so fat? — *Skinny swimmer*

If it was zero degrees today and it is going to be twice as cold tomorrow, how cold will it be?
— *Paul, Galway*

If you grab an electric fence on purpose, does it still count as a shock?
— *Curious Mary*

Q —

God created Adam & Eve and they had two children, Cain & Abel. How did the rest of us get here? Scary!

A —

The bible says that after Cain killed his brother Abel, he left Eden and found a wife 'east of Eden'. This indicates that there were other humans on the planet at the time of Adam and Eve. The story of the creation of Adam is not meant to be literal but a parable for the creation of mankind. Adam was not the first man but the first man with an awareness of God.

Q —

Why is one corner missing off all 'phone sim chips?

A —

They will only fit into the 'phone one way, therefore they cannot be put in upside down!

Q —

Ray, what was the name of the Italian inventor who was recently named the true inventor of the telephone?

A —

Antonio Meucci was born in Florence in 1808. He left Italy in 1845 and emigrated to the USA. His research into possible medical uses of electricity soon led him to realise that the human voice could be transmitted through wire. Although Meucci firmly believed that his inventions would one day make himself and his wife rich he was unable to afford to take out a patent on his 'teletrophone'. Instead, he sold the prototypes to a telegraph company. They in turn gave them to Alexander Graham Bell, who eventually patented the invention of the telephone. On 15th June 2002 the US Congress officially recognised Antonio Meucci as the inventor of the telephone, 113 years after he died in poverty in New York City.

Q —

My Irish friends and I all learned at school that Spring began in February, Summer in May, Autumn in August and Winter in November. Our English friends are telling us that Spring begins on 21st March, Summer in June, Autumn in September and Winter in December. Can you please help us to clear it up?

A —

Technically your English friends are correct! The four traditional seasons in the Northern Hemisphere are marked by the movement of the sun. Spring starts when the sun is directly over the equator, going south to north; this is the vernal equinox. Summer begins when the sun is farthest north, i.e. the summer solstice. The beginning of autumn is when the sun is directly over the equator, going north to south; this is the autumnal equinox. Winter starts when the sun is farthest south, the winter solstice. Although all these events occur on or about the 21st of a month, the dates do vary from year to year.

The First of February, St Brigid's Day, celebrates the beginning of new growth and is usually considered to be the first day of spring in Ireland.

Q —

Ray, can you tell me please who was the last man to walk on the moon?

A —

Believe it or not, the last man to set foot on the moon did so over thirty years ago. On 16th December 1972, as part of the Apollo 17 mission, astronaut Gene Cernan stepped onto the moon's surface. He remains the last person to have done so.

Q —

What is a light year?

A —

A light year is a unit of distance. It is the distance that light can travel in one year at a velocity of about 300,000 kilometres per second. This means that a light year is equal to 9,500,000,000 (nine and a half million million) kilometres!

Q —

Why does the sun turn red?

A ▬

Because of the curvature of the Earth, the light of the rising and setting sun passes a greater distance through our atmosphere than when the sun is directly overhead. The atmosphere acts as a filter, preventing transmission of the blue portion of the spectrum but allowing the longer, red wavelengths to pass through. Thus we see the rising and setting sun as a red disc.

Q ▬

Can you tell me how self-cleaning glass works because it's wrecking my head?

A ▬

The secret is the titanium oxide used in the manufacture of self-cleaning glass. When water hits standard glass it 'beads up' and runs off in rivulets, leaving streaks and spots. However, in self-cleaning glass, the titanium oxide attracts the water and causes it to run down the glass in a continuous sheet. This pushes off dirt particles and diffuses dust across the window, rather than clumping it together. This glass can even clean itself without water. Once it is exposed to ultraviolet rays from sunlight the titanium oxide acts as a catalyst, slowly breaking down organic dirt into carbon dioxide and water vapour.

Q —

How many knots are there in one mile per hour?

A —

The speed of boats, ships and planes is measured in knots. One knot is equivalent to one nautical mile per hour or 6,076 feet per hour. There are 5,280 feet in a mile. Therefore one knot is equivalent to 1.1508 miles per hour. A nautical mile is based on the circumference of the earth, which is 21,600 nautical miles, 24,857 miles or 40,003 kilometres. Look at the equator as a circle, which is divided into 360 degrees, each degree being divided into 60 minutes. One minute of arc on the surface of the planet is equal to one nautical mile.

Q —

Ray, do stalagmites go up or down?

A —

A stalagmite is a conical pillar rising from a limestone cave floor. A stalactite is a conical hanging pillar in a limestone cave. Both are formed from deposits from ground water seeping through and dripping from the cave's roof.

Q —

When the father goes out to the pub at night he usually says, 'I'm going for a quart'. Big debate about how many pints in a quart. Can you help?

A —

The British Imperial measure 'quart' is equal to two pints or 1.136 litres. A quart is one quarter of a gallon, and a gallon is eight pints.

Q —

On the last track of Robbie Williams' album *Escapology* he asks, 'What are the holes in pens for?' So I ask you, Ray, what are the holes in pens for?

A —

Approximately 90 per cent of all pens are vented to prevent leakage. The hole in the pen barrel equalises the pressure inside the pen with the pressure outside. Pens which do not have vents contain sealed ink systems and are pressurised.

Q —

Every time I get out of my car I get a small shock. This is becoming annoying and I have created a black rubber mark on the side of my door where I am closing it with my foot! Is there any way I can prevent my daily shock?

A —

This is complicated. In short, the small shock you experience is caused by contact electrification between insulating surfaces followed by separation of those surfaces. The driver is one surface and the car seat is the other. When you sit on a car seat in dry weather the contact between your clothes and the seat's surface causes electrical charges of the material to transfer between the surfaces. This is frictional or contact charging. One surface ends up with more negative charges than positive and therefore has a negative charge imbalance. The other surface has fewer negatives than positives, so it has a positive imbalance. This is similar to what happens when you rub a balloon against your hair (what do you mean, you've never done it!) – both surfaces become electrically charged.

Nothing happens as long as you remain seated. The oppositely charged surfaces cancel each other out because they are so close together. However, when you get out of the car, you take only one polarity of charge with you while the car seat retains the opposite polarity. At the same time, the car seat causes the whole car to become charged. As you step out of the car the voltage between your body and the car can reach between 10,000 and 20,000 volts. Your shoes are probably insulating, so the charge cannot leak into the earth. As you reach to close the door the opposite polarities rejoin by leaping through the air and give you a tiny burn in the tip of your finger.

There are ways to try and prevent this happening. You can avoid wearing materials which seem to aggravate the problem, usually wool and most man-made fabrics, or you could stop wearing clothes at all! Skin is reasonably conductive so it won't create charge separation when placed against your car seat – and as we go to press there are still no penalty points for nude driving! More usefully, you could develop the habit of holding your car keys as you leave the car and touching the door handle with the tip of the key. The spark will still jump, but it will not hurt you as it will be blasting the tip of your key and not your finger.

Q —

There are two or three things you can see from space that are man-made. One is the China wall. Can you help us with the others?

A —

The assertion that the Great Wall of China is the only man-made structure which can be seen from space is in fact a global myth. From a low orbit of the earth many artificial objects are visible on earth, e.g. highways, railways, cities, fields of crops and even some individual buildings. The Great Wall of China is one such structure which can be seen from low orbit. However, according to NASA, above an altitude of a few thousand kilometres no man-made objects are visible and certainly nothing specific can be seen from the moon. The earth at this distance appears as a mostly white sphere (cloud cover) with patches of blue (ocean) and yellow (desert).

Q —

Who invented the QWERTY keyboard and why?

A

The name 'QWERTY' comes from the first six letters in the top alphabet row of what is also known as the 'Universal' keyboard. It was invented by C.L. Sholes, who built the prototypes of the first commercial typewriter in a Milwaukee machine shop in the 1860s. Manual typewriters had the letters on the ends of rods called typebars, which were hung in a circle. Two letters close to each other could clash if typed in quick succession. Sholes therefore decided to place the most commonly paired letters, eg TH, at a safe distance from each other. He based his arrangement on a study of letter-pair frequency prepared by educator Amos Densmore, whose brother James was Sholes' chief financial backer. The first machines typed only capital letters but in 1878 Remington introduced the only major modification to the keyboard as we still know it today – the shift key. This enabled the machine to type lower and upper case letters by literally shifting the position of the carriage to allow the printing of either of two letters on each typebar. Modern electronic keyboards obviously do not shift mechanically but the name of the key remains the same.

Q —

What does WD-40 stand for?

A —

For the uninitiated, WD-40 is a popular anti-corrosive lubricant and cleaner. WD-40 stands for 'water displacement, 40th attempt'. The name is straight out of the laboratory book used by chemist Norm Larsen who developed WD-40 in 1953. He was trying to produce a formula to prevent corrosion, something which is accomplished by displacing water. Norm's persistence paid off when he perfected a formula on his fortieth attempt!

Q —

Why do we have leap years?

A —

The need for leap years arises from the fact that the time taken by the earth to orbit the sun (a year) is not an exact number of days, the length of the day being determined by the spin of the earth. The exact length of a year is 365.24 days. If the calendar had only 365 days in every year, the seasons, which are determined by the rotation of the earth around the sun, would drift by a quarter of a day each year. So, every four years we correct this by adding a day to February. How do you know if you are in a leap year? The rule is that a year is a leap year if it is divisible by 4. However, if the year is divisible by 100 then it is not a leap year unless it is also divisible by 400. Thus, the year 2000 was the first century leap year since 1600 as (1700, 1800 and 1900 are not divisible by 400).

Q —

What does PVC stand for?

A —

Polyvinyl chloride. This hard-wearing, synthetic resin is made by polymerising vinyl chloride.

Q —

Can you get sunburnt through glass?

A —

No. UVB rays, the ones which can cause sunburn, do not penetrate glass. However, the far more damaging UVA rays do. These can be 1,000 times more intense than UVB rays, invading deeply into underlying tissue. They can cause skin cancer and are responsible for wrinkles, dryness and age spots. Young children are particularly susceptible to UVA rays because their melanin (the skin pigment which provides some protection against the sun) is not fully developed. It is therefore important to use sun shields in car windows in the rare event of an Irish summer!

Q —

Why are there rings on the inside of a tree? I know they tell the age of the tree but how do they get there?

A —

Cambium, the cells that will become wood or bark, grows in a light layer during late spring and early summer, changing to a dark layer in later summer and early autumn. The light layer forms when the tree is growing rapidly and the dark layer is formed while the tree is growing more slowly. The growth occurs at the outside of the trunk, just below the bark. One light and one dark ring represent one year's growth. The rings can be counted to tell the age of the tree (dendrochronology). Also, because there is more growth under good conditions, growth patterns can be studied to determine the conditions a tree has lived through, e.g. forest fires, drought, insect attack, floods, etc (dendroclimatology).

Q —

What do the letters TNT stand for?

A —

Trinitrotoluene – used as an explosive.

Q —

Can it ever be 'too cold to snow'?

A —

Yes. The temperature of the air affects the amount of water vapour it can hold. Colder air holds less water than warm air. To have a significant snowfall you need significant water vapour in the air. At temperatures well below freezing there is not enough water in the air to get much snow. If it is too cold the atmosphere simply cannot hold water. No water, no snow. The best example of this is Antarctica. Precipitation at the South Pole is minimal, to the extent that it is categorised as a desert!

Q —

What is a blue moon?

A —

A blue moon is the second full moon in a calendar month. They are quite rare and can occur in any month except February, which is shorter than the lunar cycle.

Q —

Was it a man by the name of Crapper who invented the toilet?

A —

This is another common myth which we just have to explode. The first valve-type flush toilet was introduced in 1738 by a man named Brondel. It has undergone a few revisions since then to become the toilet we all know and love today. Thomas Crapper was an inventor in the late 1800s who produced a number of plumbing products. He held nine patents but did not invent the toilet. Apparently some smarty pants couldn't resist making the association!

Q —

What exactly is botox?

A —

Botox is a protein toxin produced by the *Clostridium botulinum* bacterium. It is used to eliminate facial wrinkles that occur with the use of facial muscles over time. A small amount of botox is injected directly into the facial muscles and effectively inactivates these muscles, causing lines to disappear or dramatically diminish. It is used to treat crow's feet, laughter lines and forehead wrinkles. It sometimes causes a slight, temporary drooping of the eyelids. The effects of botox are temporary, lasting from three to six months.

Q —

Who invented cat's eyes?

A —

The cat's eye was invented in 1933 by Percy Shaw from Yorkshire. The story goes that he was driving on a dark, winding road on a foggy night and was saved from veering over the side of a hill by a cat whose eyes reflected his car's headlights. Inspired by his experience, Shaw invented his road safety device to mimic the reflectivity of the cat's eyes. It is an inexpensive glass and rubber reflector. Set at regular intervals in the middle of a road, cat's eyes help motorists follow an unlit road at night.

Q —

Why is gold measured in carrots?

A —

Gold quality is measured not in carrots but in carats. Each carat represents a measure of purity on a scale of one to 24. The popular jewellery quality is 14 carats, i.e. 14/24ths or 58.35% gold. Gold can be alloyed with silver, copper and zinc.

Q —

Why does the sun darken our skin and lighten the colour of our hair?

A —

Skin darkens in the sun to protect the body against the damaging effects of UV radiation. First, dead surface skin cells absorb some of the UV light.

Then cells called melanocytes start producing extra melanin, a dark pigment, which soaks up more UV light. The more UV light you encounter, the more melanin piles up and the darker your skin becomes. However, in the case of hair, UV radiation causes a chemical reaction that destroys the melanin already deposited there by the scalp skin. Thus your hair gets lighter in the sun as your skin darkens.

Q —

Is there an easy way to convert Celsius to Fahrenheit?

A —

If you are using a calculator, multiply the Celsius temperature by 1.8 and add 32. If you don't have a calculator, or only want an approximate conversion, multiply Celsius value by 2 and add 30.

Q —

Who invented the cigarette?

A —

Tobacco was first used by native American Indians who smoked it in pipes for medicinal and ceremonial purposes. Although Christopher Columbus brought some tobacco leaves and seeds back to Europe at the end of the fifteenth century, it was not until some sixty years later that explorers and diplomats like Frenchman Jean Nicot – after whom nicotine is named – began to popularise its use. It was introduced to France in 1556, Spain in 1559 and England in 1565. No one individual is credited with addicting entire continents to the dreaded weed!

Q —

Why does helium make your voice squeaky?

A —

The speed of sound in helium is about three times that in air. This causes the frequency of the sound produced by the voice to change. What happens is this – your brain selects the configuration of your vocal chords and you force air past them, causing them to vibrate and produce sound at a given frequency. Frequencies become higher as they travel through helium – and the higher the frequency, the higher the pitch.

Q —

Why is the Phillips screwdriver so called?

A —

It is named after the inventor, Henry F. Phillips, a businessman from Oregon. The shape of the Phillips screwdriver makes it self-centring and thus very efficient for production line work.

Q —

How is horsepower measured and is it different to brake horsepower?

A —

Horsepower is a unit of power equivalent to 746 watts. It was originally defined by Scottish inventor James Watt, as the amount of power required to lift 33,000 pounds through one foot in one minute, or 550 foot pounds per second. When used as a measure of a car engines performance, 'horsepower' refers to the theoretical power of the engine, before any loss of power through heat, friction or compression. On the other hand 'brake horsepower' is measured at the point where the power is actually delivered, for example at the rear axle of a truck

Q —

Is it true that superglue was developed to patch up soldiers during the Vietnam War?

A —

Superglue was invented in 1942 and was marketed initially as a remedy for cracks in ceramics and tears in leather and plastics. It is true that soldiers fighting in Vietnam were issued with tubes of superglue to instantly seal stomach wounds in battle.

Q —

Is there really such a thing as quicksand?

A —

Yes. Quicksand is the name given to a mass of sand particles supported by circulating water. It can occur near streams, beaches and estuaries. Quicksand is very dense – in fact it has a higher density that the human body and therefore cannot 'suck you under'. If you are unfortunate enough to fall into the stuff, keep still until you stop sinking and then use slow swimming motions to get yourself into a horizontal position. Once horizontal, roll yourself onto firm ground.

Q —

Why does tonic water go blue under ultra violet light?

A —

Tonic contains quinine, a substance that undergoes fluorescence when it absorbs UV light, i.e. it absorbs light of shorter (invisible) wavelengths and emits light of longer (visible) wavelengths, in this case the blue region of the spectrum.

Q —

What is talc, the main ingredient of talcum powder?

A —

Talc is hydrated magnesium silicate, found in igneous and metamorphic rocks. Its main use is in the manufacture of talcum powder.

Q —

I am looking for a book that predicts the weather from the tides and moons – I think it may be the *Farmer's Almanac*.

A —

The book you are after is *Old Moore's Almanac* and it is still published annually.

Q —

Do all hurricanes spin in the same direction or does it depend on which side of the equator you are?

A —

Hurricanes, also known as typhoons or tropical cyclones, spin in an anti-clockwise direction north of the equator and clockwise south of the equator. There are about 40-50 hurricanes worldwide each year. A typical hurricane is about 480 kilometres wide and the eye, the central part which remains calm, measures about 30-60 kilometres across.

Q —

When you stand on a beach and look out to sea, how far away is the horizon?

A —

The answer is found in a geometric equation. The distance you can see to the horizon is the square root of the product of the elevation of the eye and the diameter of the Earth. Thus, if the elevation of the eye is 1.75 metres and the diameter of the Earth is 12,714,000 metres, you can see for a distance of approximately 4,717 metres (4.7 kilometres).

Q —

How do painkillers know where the pain is?

A —

There are two main classes of painkiller, nonnarcotic and narcotic. Nonnarcotic analgesics include aspirin, paracetamol and ibuprofen. When body tissues are damaged by injury, inflammation or infection they produce prostaglandins. These are chemicals which trigger the transmission of pain signals to the brain. Nonnarcotic painkillers, except for paracetamol, act by preventing production of prostaglandins. Paracetamol works by blocking the pain impulses in the brain itself, reducing the perception of pain. Narcotic analgesics include morphine, codeine and pethidine. These mimic endorphins, substances produced by the body itself to relieve pain. They block pain impulses at specific sites, known as opiate receptors, in the brain and spinal cord. Nonnarcotic painkillers are commonly used for everyday pain, such as headache or toothache. For more severe pain a combination analgesics might be prescribed, perhaps codeine with aspirin. The most potent narcotic painkillers are used only when other preparations would be ineffective; abuse of these drugs can lead to dependence.

Q —

What do you call the bits on the ends of your shoelaces?

A —

The little metal or plastic bit that stops your shoelace from fraying is called an aglet.

Q —

On a clock with Roman numerals why is the number 4 shown as IIII, not IV?

A —

In the case of timepieces this is probably done in the cause of symmetry, the IIII counterbalancing the VIII. However, the Romans themselves used IIII into at least the second century AD and the adoption of IV is a 'Late Latin' change.

Q —

What were the Seven Wonders of the Ancient World?

A —

The only surviving Wonder of the Ancient World is the Pyramids of Egypt. The other six were: the Colossus of Rhodes, the Mausoleum at Halicarnassus (south-western Turkey), the Hanging Gardens of Babylon (near the modern city of Baghdad, Iraq), the Temple of Artemis at Ephesus (western Turkey), the Pharos of Alexandria (a lighthouse in the harbour of Alexandria, Egypt) and the Statue of Zeus in the ancient Greek city of Olympia.

Q —

Ray. How come the glue never sticks to the inside of the container?
— *Melanie, Dundalk*

A —

Quite simply, if you use a tube of Evo-Stik or Bostik glue to stick something you expose it both to the open air and the atmosphere. Part of the contents of the glue evaporates and the remainder then bond to what ever it is attached to.

The length of time taken depends on the type of adhesive your using and also the surfaces it is sticking. Therefore if you leave the top off a container of adhesive it's exposed to the atmosphere and the hardening process starts, resulting in the glue sticking to the inside of the tube.

Q —

Ray, what's the story with those plastic balls on the electrical cables over motorways and roads round the country?

— Helen, Johnstown

The good people at the ESB marketing department tell us the reason.

A —

There are two reasons we place these orange spheres and sometimes discs on our electricity lines where they pass over roads or near estuaries. One reason is to protect birds from damage where they could actually crash into the lines and hurt themselves. What we have found over the years is that bird flight paths tend to be fairly constant. They tend to use the same routes regularly and geese and swans can sometimes be fairly short sighted; so we wanted to warn them in due time that the power lines are there.

The other reason is that many helicopter pilots use the national motorway and road system as a navigation aid when they are travelling around the county. Because of that, if they are flying low there obviously would be a danger that they could hit one of our power lines if they are close to a motorway.

We want to give them due warning and enable them to avoid any power lines nearby.

Do Mexican waves go in reverse in the southern hemisphere? — *Bored in Dublin*

Why do men wear bum bags when on holiday but not at home for the same purpose?
— *Anon*

Q —

Where and when did Steve Collins fight Chris Eubank?

A —

Collins beat Eubank in the Green Glens Arena in Millstreet, Co. Cork on March 18th 1995 and he defeated him again on September 9th of the same year, this time the fight took place in Páirc Uí Chaoimh. Collins retired in 1997, still retaining his WBO Super Middleweight Title. He fought 39 professional fights and won 36.

Q —

One of the stands behind the goals at Anfield is called the KOP. I heard that this stands for King Over Pope! Is there any truth in this?

A —

No. What is now known as the Kop was originally called the Oakfield Road Embankment or Walton Breck Bank. It was renamed in 1906 after the battle of Spion Kop, fought in 1900 during the Boer War. The Boers had inflicted a heavy defeat on the British army and many of the soldiers killed came from the north west of England.

Q —

How did Nike, Adidas and Reebok get their names?

A —

Nike is the ancient Greek goddess of victory and also a symbol for the Olympic Games. Adidas was founded by Adolph (Adi) Dassler. Reebok is named after a South African antelope.

Q —

Did you know that Adi Dasler's brother started Puma?

A —

Of course! Rudolf Dassler founded Puma in Germany in 1948. His brother Ade was the founder of Adidas.

Q —

Who is the Nally Stand in Croke Park called after?

A —

Patrick William Nally was the inspiration for the GAA rather than its founder. At a time (late nineteenth century) when sport was the privilege of the land-owning class, Nally organised the National Sports of Mayo in 1879 and 1880. These meetings were open to all-comers and Nally persuaded Charles Stewart Parnell to be patron for them. The success of these fixtures led to the founding of the Gaelic Athletic Association, although Nally was a prisoner in Mountjoy when this happened and remained there until his death in 1891.

Q —

What is the fastest soccer goal ever scored?

A —

There are a number of claimants around the world for this distinction but the two most likely contenders are Colin Cowperthwaite and Ricardo Olivera. Cowperthwaite is the official record holder for the fastest goal in the world in 3.58 seconds. This was scored in 1979 when he was playing for Barrow. However, it is claimed that Olivera, playing for Uraguay in 1998, scored in only 2.8 seconds.

Q —

Did you ever hear of a Durex glove and what is it used for?

A —

Brand names can cause confusion when used in different parts of the world. In Australia, Durex is an adhesive tape; in this part of the world it is a brand of condom! However, it is also the name of sports gloves made for motorcyclists and golfers. Be sure you know what you are asking for!

Q —

Who was the first sportsperson to wear Nike runners?

A —

The first major athlete to wear Nike runners was Steve Prefontaine, a middle-distance runner.

Q —

Who scored the first televised 147?

A —

The first televised 147 break was completed by Steve Davis against John Spencer in the Lada Classic in Oldham, Lancashire. The date was 11th January 1982.

Q —

How long is the outside lane on a 400 metre running track?

A —

On an eight lane track the outside lane is 453.029 metres. Runners all cover the same distance in any given race as start lines are staggered.

Q —

Why are there 18 holes on a golf course?

A —

Like a lot of these things, it is an accident of history. In the early days of golf, courses did not have a standard number of holes. Then, on 5th May 1858, a set of rules was issued by the Royal and Ancient Golf

Club at St Andrews in Scotland. It so happened that the course had 18 holes and so the rules stipulated that: 'one round of the links or 18 holes is reckoned a match'. Over time, this became the standard around the world.

Q —

In pool, what is a massé shot?

A —

The massé is a technique that causes the cue ball to follow a curved path. The shot is accomplished by tilting the axis of the ball so that it spins to the inside of the desired curve, against the grain of the felt. Using this technique it is possible to make a tight turn around a number of balls.

Q —

What do the letters KNVB stand for on the Dutch national football jerseys?

A —

'Koninklijke Nederlandse Voetbal Bond', i.e. Royal Dutch Football Association.

Q —

Why are the different shots in golf called after birds?

A —

In golf the term birdie refers to a shot that is one under par, an eagle is two under par and an albatross (or double eagle) is three under par. In nineteenth century American slang 'bird' was used to describe anything that was excellent or wonderful. The term was adopted by golfers to describe a good shot – and it stuck.

Q —

Who was the first Black football player in England?

A —

Arthur Wharton, born in the Gold Coast (now Ghana) in 1865, became the world's first Black professional footballer. He made his debut appearance for Darlington in 1884 and later played for Preston North End, Rotherham, Sheffield United and others. Professional football did not carry the financial rewards of today in the late 1800s and Wharton ended his years as a coal miner. His grave in Edlington, near Doncaster, was

unmarked until 1997 when 'Football Unites –
Racism Divides' erected a headstone to
commemorate a great Black athlete.

Q –

How did the term 'The Ashes' originate?

A –

August 1882 the Australian cricket team beat
England at the Oval in London in a match that is
still regarded as one of the best ever. This was an
ignominious defeat for the English and *The
Sporting Times* published an Obituary to English
Cricket, which ended with the words: 'The body
will be cremated and the ashes taken to Australia'.
The defeated English team decided to travel to
Australia in an attempt to retrieve their honour.
The first game was played in Adelaide and was
drawn. At the end of it the English captain, Ivo
Bligh, said: 'I have come to retrieve the ashes of
English cricket.' He was later presented with an
urn containing the ashes of either the ball or the
bails used in that match.

Q —

How wide is a soccer goal?

A —

The distance between goalposts is 8 yards (7.32 metres). The distance from the lower edge of the crossbar to the ground is 8 feet (2.44 metres).

Q —

Can you name Ireland's and Europe's largest golf complexes?

A —

The Deer Park in Dublin is Ireland's largest golf complex with 66 holes, including two full 18-hole courses. St Andrew's Links in Scotland is the largest golf complex in Europe. It has five 18-hole courses and one 9-hole course.

Q —

Why is 147 always quoted as a maximum break in snooker when it is possible to make a 155 break?

A —

147 (15 reds and 15 blacks) is generally accepted as a maximum break. However, if a free ball is awarded after a foul, it is possible to achieve a 155 break (16 reds and 16 blacks).

Q —

Was Dawson Stelfox the first Irishman to climb Mount Everest?

A —

Yes, in 1993.

Q —

In poker, what are the top five hands?

A —

The top five hands and your chances of acquiring them are: Royal Flush (1 in 650,000), Straight Flush (1 in 65,000), Four of a Kind (1 in 4,000), Full House (1 in 700), Flush (1 in 500).

Q —

What happens in soccer if the ball hits the referee and goes into one of the goals?

A —

It is better if the referee and his assistant referees stay well clear of the goal as they are considered to be part of the field of play. This means that if a ball deflects off one of them into the goal, it is allowed!

Q —

Who was the first Formula One woman driver?

A —

The first woman to race in Formula One was Maria-Teresa de Filippis. The Italian woman raced in three Grand Prix for Maserati, her best finish being 10th in Belgium in 1958.

Q —

Where does the name 'pool' come from (as in a form of billiards)?

A —

It comes from the French word 'poule', meaning 'hen'. During the seventeenth century hens were used as stakes and prizes in various forms of gambling.

Q —

How many All-Ireland medals did Kevin Moran win with Dublin?

A —

Kevin Moran is the only person to have won GAA All-Ireland senior football medals and FA Cup medals. The All-Ireland medals were won with Dublin in 1976 and 1977. The FA Cup medals were won with Manchester United in 1983 and 1985. He was also capped for Ireland 71 times and scored six international goals.

Q —

What does BMX stand for?

A —

BMX is short for bicycle motocross, a sport which developed in California in the early 1970s.

Q —

How many caps did Eamon Dunphy get for Ireland?

A —

Eamon Dunphy was capped 23 times between 1966 and 1977.

Q —

Is it true that two basketballs can fit into the hoop side by side?

A —

Yes. The diameter of a basketball is nine inches (23 centimetres). The hoop and net through which it must pass are 18 inches (46 centimetres) in diameter.

Q —

Who won the first soccer World Cup?

A —

Thirteen countries participated in the very first World Cup in Uruguay in 1930. The host country won the final, beating Argentina 4-2.

Q —

Who took the five penalties against Romania during Italia '90?

A —

Will we ever forget the match which took Ireland to the quarter finals of the World Cup? After 30 minutes of extra time the game went to penalties. The first four were taken and scored by Kevin Sheedy, Ray Houghton, Andy Townsend and Tony Cascarino. Packie Bonner then saved the shot from Timofte. Dave O'Leary stepped up to the spot and scored the winning goal.

Q —

In which year was the offside rule introduced into soccer?

A —

The first offside rule was introduced in the 'Cambridge' rules of 1848, whereby three opposition players were required to be between the forward player and the goal. In 1925 this was modified by the FA to require two opposition players between the forward player and the goal.

Q —

What do the words 'audere est facere' mean on the Spurs team crest?

A —

They are Latin for 'to dare is to do'.

Q —

How many times did Crossmaglen Rangers with the All-Ireland Club Championship?

A —

Three times: 1997, 1999 and 2000.

Q —

Why is Hill 16 so called?

A —

That part of Croke Park, the biggest GAA stadium in Ireland, which is known as Hill 16 was built from the rubble resulting from the bombing of the GPO in Sackville Street (now O'Connell Street) and surrounding buildings during the 1916 Easter Rising. It was built as a memorial to the Rising and those who lost their lives.

I am an aspiring superhero, tell me can I be arrested for wearing my underpants outside my trousers? — *C.Kent*

Ray, where do ice cream vans go in winter?
— *99 fan*

Ray and gang, did everyone else's parents use the 'syllable bumslap' method when giving out? 'Don't (slap) you (slap) ever (slap) do (slap) that (slap) again (slap)!' — *Darren, Claregalway*

Q —

Hi Ray, there were 13 *Mr Benn* episodes but I only know the names of a few of them – please can you find out the names of all 13?

A —

They were: The Pirate, The Spaceman, The Magic Carpet, The Clown, The Wizard, The Cowboy, The Diver, The Zoo Keeper, The Balloonist, The Caveman, The Cook, The Hunter, The Red Knight.

Q —

What was the name of the cat in *The Smurfs*?

A —

The cat's name was Azrael. He belonged to Gargamel, an evil sorcerer, and he was every bit as unpleasant as his master!

Q —

Does anyone know the name of a kids show that was on years ago, it had a girl called Vicky who was a robot that her dad had made? It's been bugging me for ages.

A —

The show was called *Small Wonder* and its star was V.I.C.I. (Voice Input Child Identicant), a robot built by cybernetics genius Ted Lawson. In order to test his creation's performance in the real world Ted and his wife legally adopt the robot who becomes Victoria 'Vicky' Ann Smith-Lawson. She attends Grant Junior High School where her exploits cause consternation among her fellow students.

Q —

Who lived in Cockleshell Bay?

A —

Robin and Rosie. *Cockleshell Bay* was first shown on ITV in 1980. At least 100 episodes were made of this clay model type animation.

Q —

Could you please tell me the name of the cartoon that was on *The Den* years ago? When the man said 'Strength of the bear' he would get that strength and so on.

A —

BraveStarr was the name of this cartoon series. Set in the 24th century, the cartoon starred Marshal BraveStarr of the planet New Texas. He could call upon the powers of nature to help him maintain law and order, e.g. strength of the bear, speed of the puma, eyes of the hawk, ears of the wolf. This cartoon had a number of other wonderfully named characters, including Deputy Fuz, Tex Hex, Handlebar, Outlaw Scuzz and Dingo Dan.

Q —

There was a cartoon years ago called *Hong Kong Phooey*. It had a cat or a dog who solved problems. Please, please tell me the name of the animal. It's driving me mad!

A —

Penrod Pooch is a dog who works as a janitor at police headquarters. However, when evil threatens he grabs his mask and kimono and transforms into martial arts superhero Hong Kong Phooey.

Q —

Did I dream it or was there a TV show in the 80s called *Educating Marmalade*?

A —

You didn't dream it. Marmalade Atkins was the naughtiest girl in the world!

Q —

Who is the voice of the storyteller in *Noddy*?

A —

It is the voice of Richard Briers. His most famous TV role was as Tom Good in *The Good Life*, playing opposite Felicity Kendall as his wife, Barbara.

Q —

What is the name of the evil frog in *Danger Mouse*?

A —

Danger Mouse's arch-enemy is the evil Baron Silas Greenback, a megalomaniac frog. Danger Mouse and his faithful hamster sidekick, Penfold, battle constantly to save the planet from Greenback and his henchman crow, Stiletto.

Q —

Who was Morph's friend?

A —

Morph's pale friend is Chaz.

Q —

Can you tell me and the people who don't believe me that there was a kids' programme called *The Moomins*?

A —

The Moomins were created by Tove Jansson, a Swedish children's author. Her books have been translated into 34 languages and were made into an animated series in 1980. Currently there is an internet petition to get the production company, Film Polski, to release *The Moomins* in DVD. For the uninitiated, Moomin Trolls are small, shy and fat and live in the forest of Finland.

Q —

In the kids' show *Captain Pugwash*, was there a character called Master Bates?

A —

Despite the urban myths, there was no character with this name. Nor was there a Seaman Staines or a Roger the Cabin Boy aboard the good ship *Black Pig*. Captain Pugwash's real crew were Master Mate, Tom the Cabin Boy, Pirate Barnabas and Pirate Willy.

Q —

What was the name of the band in the *Muppet Show*, the one that Animal played the drums in?

A —

The band was called 'Dr Teeth and the Electric Mayhem'. It featured Animal on drums and Floyd on guitar.

Q —

Who were the two old guys that used to sit in the balcony seat on the *Muppet Show*?

A —

The two old guys were Statler and Waldorf.

Q —

Which cartoon was Snaggle Puss in?

A —

Snagglepuss originally appeared in 1959 as a minor character on episodes of *Quick Draw McGraw*, *Augie Doggie* and *Snooper & Blabber*. He proved to be so popular that he was given his own segment on *The Yogi Bear Show* in 1961. Snagglepuss's famous catchphrases were 'Exit stage left' and 'Heavens to Murgatroid'. His unforgettable voice was provided by Daws Butler, Hanna-Barbera's most prolific voice artist. Butler was also the voice of Yogi Bear, Huckleberry Hound, Mr Jinks and Dixie, Quick Draw McGraw and many others.

Q —

Are there any female Umpa Lumpas in *Charley & the Chocolate Factory*. Thanks.

A —

None! The Umpa Lumpas are the little orange men who work in the Chocolate Factory.

Q —

What was the name of the big lads in *Fraggle Rock*?

A —

The 'big lads' are the Gorgs, hairy giants who think they rule the universe.

Q —

Who was the bad guy in *Wanderly Wagon*?

The baddie was Dr Astro, played by Frank Kelly.

Q —

What was the horse's name in *Wanderly Wagon*?

A —

Pádraig.

Q —

Could you find out why Mr Sanders is above Winnie the Pooh's door?

A —

Sanders is definitely not Winnie the Pooh's surname. Mr Sanders was the previous resident of Pooh's house and the sign was simply left behind when he moved out.

Q —

Could you please settle a long running bet between me and my friends who think the original series of *Flipper* was based in Australia. I say it was America!

A —

You are right, *Flipper* was based in Florida.

Q —

Can you name Top Cat's gang?

A —

They were: Top Cat, Choo Choo, Benny the Ball, Spook, Fancy Fancy and The Brain. They spent their days trying to outsmart Officer Dibble.

Q —

Ray and the gang. I know this is an old one, but I still don't know the answer. How the hell do they get the writing into the sticks of rock? And how come it goes all the way through?
— *Colm and Tom, Kilkenny*

We went to the experts for this one. The most famous rock in the world is made in Blackpool, and Coronation are the longest established makers of Blackpool rock still operating. Here's how they make their rock.

A —

At Coronation, we've been making rock for over 75 years now. However, it is a little bit difficult to explain over the phone, but bear with me and I'll try to go through it.

We start by boiling up sugar and glucose. That gets boiled up to about 300 degrees Fahrenheit. We then pour that out on concrete tables, which are water-cooled and as the mixture cools, its gets solid, like very thick treacle and then eventually it gets hard.

To make the letters we basically take some of the hot toffee as it cools down and add colours – say we were putting red letters through the rock, we'd add some red colouring. The letters are created using long strips of toffee around one metre long. The letters are built up inside a round mould. When all the letters are in place, the white toffee mixture is poured in. And this is all put together and you end up with a really big sausage shape piece of rock weighing about 60 kilos, 1.3 metres long maybe and 60 centimetres in diameter. This piece is then put in a machine and its extruded or stretched down to the traditional size of rock (normally 25 centimetres long and about 2 centimetres thick). This final part of the operation is done by hand. As the original cylinder is reduced in size so too is the lettering encased within it. So we end up with a small but perfectly formed 'Blackpool Rock' that runs right through the centre of the rock.

TRADITION

Ray, is it true that in County Leitrim it is traditional to start every family meal with a verse of Iron Maiden's 'Run to the Hills'?
— *Paul, Tullamore*

Q —

There are Aran sweaters in Ireland and Scotland. Which is the original?

A —

The patterns used in traditional Aran sweaters were first recorded in Scotland in the early ninth century. These patterns reflected the interweaving designs engraved on the great Pictish standing stones of prehistory. The sweaters worn along Ireland's Atlantic seaboard appear to be a fairly short-lived tradition as there is no record of them before the twentieth century.

Q —

Why is the stork associated with babies?

A —

This is a Scandinavian tradition. Mothers would tell their children that a new baby was brought by the stork and that the stork had bitten the mother, hence the reason that she might be in need of rest! There were a number of reasons for choosing the stork. It would often nest in chimneys and so was almost one of the household. It is also a very affectionate and loyal bird, mating for life.

Q —

Why is it considered lucky to 'touch wood'?

A —

People touch wood to keep bad luck away. The origin of this superstition is thought to be associated with the wooden cross upon which Jesus was crucified. Wooden crucifix necklaces would be worn as good luck charms and over time wood became associated with safety and good fortune.

Q —

Who wrote the 'Happy Birthday' song?

A —

Two sisters, Mildred and Patty Hill, both taught at the same Kentucky kindergarten. In 1893 they published a collection of *Song Stories of the Kindergarten*, which included a song entitled 'Good Morning to All'. More than three decades later, in 1924, Robert H. Coleman wrote and published a second verse, 'Happy Birthday to You', using the Hill sisters' tune and original first verse without permission. The song we all now know as 'Happy

Birthday to You' quickly became popular while the sisters' first verse and title disappeared. Although Mildred had died in 1916, Patty and another sister, Jessica, sued Mr Coleman and proved that they owned the tune.

Q —

Why is Friday the 13th considered unlucky?

A —

There are a couple of reasons why this date is considered unlucky in Christian societies. There were thirteen people present at the Last Supper, the thirteenth being Judas, the traitor. Traditionally, it has been believed that Christ was crucified on a Friday and so the day and the number became imbued with ominous significance. Later in Christian history, on Friday 13th October 1307, the Pope and the King of France ordered a murderous purge of the Knights Templar, who were perceived to hold too much power. Their Grand Master, Jacques De Molay, was tortured and crucified. This event, more than any other, is believed to be the basis for our modern superstition surrounding Friday the 13th.

Q —

Where does the superstition of 'something old, something new, something borrowed, something blue' in relation to a bride come from?

A —

The 'old' traditionally is a personal gift from mother to daughter, a passing on of wisdom. The 'new' symbolises the new family unit formed by the bride and her groom. The 'borrowed' item should come from a happily married woman, bringing a share of marital bliss to the new couple. The 'blue' has two origins: in ancient Rome maidens wore blue-bordered robes to denote their virtue and in the Christian faith the colour is associated with the purity of the Virgin Mary.

Q —

Why the 25th December for Christmas Day?

A —

The actual date of Jesus's birth is not known but the event has been celebrated since the 4th century. During the rule of the Roman Emperor Constantine (the first Christian Emperor of

Rome) the old pagan festival of Saturnalia, which was celebrated around the time of the winter solstice, was superseded by 'Christ's Mass'. Eventually 25th December became almost universally accepted as the date on which Christmas would be celebrated, although the Eastern Orthodox Church observe 6th January (Epiphany) instead.

Q —

Could you explain the tradition of following the wren on St. Stephen's Day?

A —

The origin of this custom is uncertain but the most likely legend to have sparked it, is that St. Stephen (first Christian martyr), while hiding from his enemies in a bush, was betrayed by a chattering wren. As a punishment the wren was to be hunted and stoned like St. Stephen. The tradition of boys dressed up with blackened faces and killing the wren, which they placed on a pole, all but disappeared at the beginning of the twentieth century. It has been revived in recent years although the wrens are no longer hunted. The wren boys now consist of males and females of all ages and their processions or parades, which usually include traditional song and dance, are often in aid of charity.

Q —

Is it true that 'Silent Night' was written for the guitar?

A —

Yes. It was Christmas Eve 1818 and Austrian priest Joseph Mohr discovered that his church organ was broken and could not be repaired in time for the Christmas ceremonies. He could not face Christmas without music so he sat down and wrote three verses which could be sung by a choir with guitar accompaniment. 'Stille Nacht' was the product of necessity!

Q —

Why is St. Stephen's Day also known as Boxing Day?

A —

There are two types of boxes associated with Boxing Day. Traditionally alms boxes, or collection boxes which were placed in churches over Christmas, were opened on this day and their contents distributed to the poor and needy. In the nineteenth century the tradition was expanded when the merchant classes and employers gave their servants and employees gifts or bonuses which were distributed in, you guessed it, boxes.

Q —

Who was Good King Wenceslas?

A —

He wasn't actually a king but the Duke of Bohemia, in what is today Slovakia and the Czech Republic. He lived in the tenth century.

Q —

Why is the filling for mince pies called mincemeat when there's no meat in it?

A —

The mince pie in mediaeval times was oblong in shape, indented at the centre. The pie symbolised Christ's cradle and a small pastry doll was usually placed in the hollow. The pie was filled with minced lamb's tongue and mutton and spiced fruits. Crusaders returning from the East brought exotic

223

dried fruits and spices with them and these eventually replaced completely the meat content of the mince pie. Over time the shape of the pie also changed to become the round treat which we all know today. The only reminder of its origins is the name mincemeat, still used to describe its filling.

Q —

Who produced the first Christmas cards?

A —

The first commercial Christmas card is believed to have been designed and painted by John Calcott Horsley at the behest of Sir Henry Cole, a leading cultural light of Victorian England. The card depicted a family feast and was emblazoned with the words 'A Merry Christmas and a Happy New Year to You'.

Q —

Why do we kiss under the mistletoe?

A —

The custom of bringing mistletoe into the house dates back to the ancient Druids, who considered it to have mystical powers which would bring good luck to the household. It was also used as a symbol of friendship, hence the tradition of kissing beneath it. The original custom was to pick a berry from the mistletoe before embarking on the kiss – once all the berries were gone there would be no more kissing!

Q —

Where did the tradition of pantomime originate and why do men and women cross-dress?

A —

This one also goes back to the Roman feast of Saturnalia. Part of the craic at this mid-winter festival was for men to dress as women and women to dress as men. The modern pantomime is a legacy of the Italian 'commedia dell'arte', a tradition of improvised theatre with larger-than-life stock characters. A mix of fairy stories, folk tales and traditional plots eventually evolved into the familiar pantomime repertoire that we know today.

Q —

Where did Santa come from?

A —

St Nicholas, a 4th century Turkish bishop, was the inspiration for today's Santa Claus. He was famous for his kindness and generosity. Over time the custom became established of children putting out food for the saint on 6th December, St Nicholas's Eve, along with straw for his horse. In the morning the food and straw would be replaced by sweets and toys. St Nicholas went through some changes over the centuries, becoming Weihnachtsmann in Germany, Père Noël in France and Father Christmas in Britain. In the Netherlands he became Sinter Klass and in the 1600s was brought by Dutch settlers to America. The name eventually evolved into Santa Claus. In 1823 Clement C. Moore wrote the poem 'A Visit From St Nicholas', known today as 'The Night Before Christmas'. In it, Santa's horse was exchanged for a reindeer-powered sleigh. Moore also described Santa as a jolly, rotund figure and illustrator Thomas Nast gave him substance.

What does the red and white pole outside a barber's shop signify?

For many centuries barbers did more than just cut hair. They also performed minor surgery, tooth extractions and bloodletting. After such operations the bloodied bandages would be hung on a staff and placed outside the barber's premises as an advertisement. The leeches, used for bloodletting, are long gone but a more hygienic version of the barber's pole is still in use today.

Q —

How long has Speaker's Corner existed in London's Hyde Park?

A —

Since 1872 Speaker's Corner has been available on Sundays to anyone who wishes to air their views in public. It is close to the old hanging site of Tyburn and it is believed that the tradition of free speech at this spot evolved from the right of a condemned person to make a final address.

Ray, do Eskimos have to insure their homes against fire? — *Paula*

How come Ireland doesn't have a space programme. I mean, India has one? It's hardly rocket science. — *Angela, Glasnevin*

Q —

Who made the first ascent of Mt. Everest without the use of oxygen?

A —

Peter Habeler, an Austrian, and Reinhold Messner, an Italian, jointly share this distinction. They successfully climbed Mt. Everest without bottled oxygen in 1975.

Q —

Where is the biggest and oldest tree in Ireland?

A —

They are not one and the same! The tallest tree in Ireland is a Douglas fir in the Powerscourt Estate in Co. Wicklow. It is – wait for it – 56 metres high! The biggest tree (the tree with the largest girth) is a Monterey Cypress in Innishannon, Co. Cork, with a circumference of 12 metres. The oldest tree is over one thousand years old. It is a Yew tree in Bunclody, Co. Wexford.

Q —

Hey Ray, who is McGillicuddy and does he really smell that bad!?

A —

The Magillicuddy Reeks are of course the highest mountain range in Ireland and are located in Co. Kerry. The MacGillicuddys, after whom the mountains are named, were a branch of the O'Sullivan clan and were chiefs of a territory in the barony of Dunkerron. There are no historical records relating to their personal hygiene!

Q —

Where is the biggest fountain in the world?

A —

Suntec City, Singapore. It is known as the Fountain of Wealth. It is three storeys high and has two underground storeys of shops and restaurants.

Q —

How did Leopardstown come by its name?

A —

From mediaeval times to the eighteenth century, Leopardstown in South Dublin, was known as Leperstown. From at least the early thirteenth century the lands in this area were owned by the religious order who ran the Leper Hospital of St Stephen in Dublin, on the site now occupied by Mercer's Hospital. Some historians have suggested that Leperstown may have been the site of an auxiliary home of lepers but there is no documentary evidence to support this.

Q —

Is there a place in Cork called Newtwopothouse?

A —

Yes, in Mallow.

Q —

How is the Ice Hotel heated?

A —

The 'Ishotellet' is built every December in Jukkasjärvi, Sweden, 160 kilometres inside the Arctic Circle. It is a single-storey structure made entirely of ice, which begins to melt sometime in May. Only the very hardy should consider reserving a room as there is no heating! The hotel is warmed by candles and human metabolism. The other bit of bad news is that the bar doesn't serve beer because it would freeze!

Q —

Which is the highest mountain in Europe?

A —

Mount Elbrus in Southern Russia, at 5,642 metres, is the highest mountain in Europe. Mont Blanc, in the French Alps, is the highest mountain in Western Europe at 4,807 metres.

Q —

Is the Vatican a country and does it have its own euro?

Yes, the Holy See or Vatican City is an independent state and it does have its own euro. All the Vatican coins are identical in style, depicting Pope John Paul II facing left.

Q —

Is the Vatican really the smallest country in the world?

A —

At only 0.44 square kilometres in area, the Vatican City is indeed the smallest country in the world.

Q —

What's the population of Dundlak?

A —

The population according to the 2002 Census is 27,385. It is the second biggest town in Ireland. For your information here are the 10 biggest towns in Ireland.

1.	Drogheda	28,333
2.	Dundalk	27,385
3.	Swords	27,175
4.	Bray	26,244
5.	Tralee	20,375
6.	Ennis	18,830
7.	Sligo	18,473
8.	Naas	18,288
9.	Newbridge	15,749
10.	Clonmel	15,739

Statistics from CSO Census 2002 (figures exclude environs)

Where is the river Saile which features in a Dubliners' song?

The river Saile, mentioned in the song 'Weile Weile Waila' is today known as the Poddle. It was previously called the Tiber and also the river Salach (meaning 'dirty'), from which is derived Saile. The Poddle formed a natural defence on the south and east sides of Dublin Castle and at one time provided much of the drinking water for Dublin's inhabitants. It now flows under the grounds of Dublin Castle from Ship Street Gate to the Chapel Royal and the Undercroft and enters the Liffey at Wellington Quay. The peaty water of the Poddle coloured the Black Pool after which the Vikings named Dublin.

Q —

Why is New York called 'The Big Apple'?

A —

New York City was first referred to as 'The Big Apple' in *The Wayfarer in New York*, a 1909 book edited by Edward S. Martin. In attempting to illustrate the Midwest's attitude to the city he wrote: 'New York (was) merely one of the fruits of that great tree whose roots go down in the Mississippi Valley, and whose branches spread from one ocean to the other . . . (But) the big apple (New York) gets a disproportionate share of the national sap'.

The term lost the begrudging overtones when popularised in the 1920s by sports writer John J. Fitzgerald, whose horse-racing column in the *New York Morning Telegraph* was called Around the Big Apple. The phrase was also widely used by jazz musicians of the 1930s and '40s, who considered 'playing the Big Apple' to be the pinnacle of success. The Big Apple became an internationally recognised nickname after it was used in the 1970s in a tourism campaign for New York City.

Q —

Which is the largest island in the world. Is it Australia or Greenland?

A —

Greenland is the largest island at 2,175,590 km^2. Although Australia is technically an island, its huge size (7,692,030km^2) means that it is considered to be a continent.

Q —

What is the biggest country without a coastline?

A —

Kazakhstan is the world's ninth largest country but the largest landlocked. It covers 2,670,000 km^2 and is bordered by Russia, China, the Kyrgyz Republic, Uzbekistan, Turkmenistan and the landlocked Caspian Sea.

Q —

Which is the largest lake in the world?

A

At 436,000 square kilometres it is the Caspian Sea.

Q —

Is New England a state or a city?

A —

Neither. New England is the collective name given to the six states of the north-eastern USA. They are Maine, New Hampshire, Vermont, Massachusetts, Rhode Island and Connecticut. New England is strongly associated with America's colonial past and the American Revolution began there.

Q —

What is the total square mileage of the 32 counties?

A —

The 32 counties consist of the 26 counties of the Irish Republic and the six counties of Northern Ireland. Their total square mileage is 32,593, of which 31,557 square miles are land and 1,036 square miles are water.

Q —

Why is Clare called the Banner County?

A —

In the nineteenth century the carrying of banners to political meetings became widespread in Clare and they were used to welcome Daniel O'Connell to the Clare election of 1828. In addition, there was a strong tradition of trade guilds having their own banners. Bakers, butchers, coopers, shoe-makers, cartwrights, stone-cutters and many others vied with each other to produce the most elaborate banners. At the inauguration of the O'Connell monument in Ennis in 1865, thirteen different guilds carried banners.

Q —

What is the capital of The Netherlands?

A —

Amsterdam is the capital. The Hague is the seat of government.

Q

Why is the London police headquarters called 'Scotland Yard'?

A

The headquarters of the London Metropolitan Police Force, and in particular its Criminal Investigation Department, have been known as Scotland Yard since the force was set up in 1829. The name derives from the original site of the police HQ which had been used as a residence by visiting Scottish monarchs in mediaeval times. In 1890 the HQ were moved to new buildings on the Thames Embankment which were known as New Scotland Yard. The current housing for the Metropolitan Police, near the Houses of Parliament, was opened in 1967.

Q

How many continents are there?

A

It is generally accepted that there are seven continents: Africa, Antarctica, Asia, Europe, North America, South America and Australia/Oceania (formerly known as Australia or Australasia and comprising Australia and the islands of the SW Pacific).

Q —

Where in the world is Pontchartrain?

A —

The Lakes of Pontchartrain, as immortalised in the famous song, are in Louisiana. They are the site of the longest over-water bridge in the world, known as The Lake Pontchartrain Causeway, which is crossed by approximately 30,000 vehicles every weekday.

Q —

Which is the largest county in Ireland?

A —

In terms of area, Cork is the largest county at 7,457 km^2. The largest county in Northern Ireland is Tyrone at 3,155 km^2.

Q —

Who was Sally and why is there a Gap named after her?

A —

For the uninitiated the Sally Gap is a high crossroads in the Wicklow Mountains. Its Irish name is 'Bearnas na Diallaite', meaning 'Gap of the Saddle', the saddle being a mountain pass. Sally is therefore a corruption of saddle.

Q —

Why is Holland also called The Netherlands and how come the people are Dutch and not Hollish?

A —

Netherlands simply means low-lying territory – one third of the country is below sea level. It is one of The Low Countries. The Netherlands used to be a series of principalities, of which Holland was one. Holland today consists of the two western coastal provinces along the North Sea. Some other Dutch provinces have familiar names, e.g. Utrecht and Zeeland. When these principalities first came together Holland was the most powerful, which is probably why the country is often named after it. 'Nederlanders' is the Dutch word for people from The Netherlands!

Q —

How big is the Phoenix Park?

A —

Most people know of the Phoenix Park's claim to fame as the largest enclosed urban park in Europe. It covers an area of 1,760 acres (712 hectares). One hectare is 10,000 square metres.

Q —

How long is Ireland?

A —

From Malin Head in the north to Mizzen Head in the south is a distance of 489 kilometres. If you are interested in its width, from Slyne Head in the west to Howth Head in the east is 272 kilometres.

Q —

Where is the biggest waterfall in Ireland?

A —

Ireland's tallest waterfall is Powerscourt Falls in Co. Wicklow. The water drops 106 metres, making it the third tallest waterfall in the British Isles.

Q —

How did New Zealand get its name?

A —

The spelling was originally Nieuw Zeeland and the name was given by Dutch geographers in honour of the Dutch province of Zeeland. They had already used the name Nieuw Holland for Australia!

Q —

How many countries are there?

A —

There are 191 members of the United Nations but there are another two states which are not members. These are Vatican City and Taiwan. The Vatican has chosen to stay outside of the United Nations but Taiwan is not universally recognised as an independent country because China, a Security Council member, claims that it is merely a Chinese province.

Q —

What is the most spoken language in the world?

A —

The top three are: Chinese (Mandarin) – 885 million speakers, Spanish – 332 million speakers, English – 322 million speakers.

Q

In Birmingham Airport there are Wudu facilities. What are these?

A

Wudu is a ritual cleansing or ablution carried out by people of the Muslim faith before prayer. It is carried out five times a day. The facilities at Birmingham Airport provide an opportunity for Muslims to observe their religious practices.

TRANSPORT

Why are toilet windows in aeroplanes always frosted over – are they afraid of geese peeping in?
— *Dermot, Dundalk*

Whenever there's a fire drill, we're always told to walk in an orderly fashion, so why is that wee guy on the emergency exit sign running?
— *Anne, Sligo*

Q —

What do the initials MG stand for?

A —

They stand for Morris Garages. The famous badge was introduced in 1924.

Q —

What does 'aero' mean on the back of the Saab 9-3?

A —

Saab prides itself on its background in aviation and has always paid great attention to the aerodynamics of its designs. The 'aero' on the 9-3 models refers to its superior aerodynamic properties – Saab claim to have dramatically reduced lift forces, thus giving greater stability at high speed.

Q —

How many countries other than Ireland and Britain use right-hand drive?

A —

There are another 62 countries which use right-hand drive vehicles and drive on the left-hand side of the road. These include Australia, India, Japan, New Zealand, Pakistan, South Africa, Thailand, Uganda and Zimbabwe.

Q —

Which motor company introduced electric windows?

A —

Daimler were the first to use electric windows in cars in 1948.

Some other interesting firsts were: electric car heater – 1890, electronic fuel injection – 1966, electric turn indicators – 1938 and car radio – 1929.

Q —

What do the letters SF on the Ferrari flag stand for?

A —

They stand for 'scuderia' Ferrari. The term 'scuderia' dates back to the Middle Ages. It referred to a place where racing horses were kept. Now these racing horses are racing cars and the term Scuderia Ferrari remains.

Q —

Where did the Mercedes three-pointed star come from?

A —

Gottlieb Daimler, whose Daimler Phoenix was marketed in France under the name Mercedes, designed the three-pointed star to symbolise the growth of his business into land, sea and air transport. Karl Benz used a cogwheel, and later a laurel wreath, to symbolise the superior engineering in his cars. In 1926 the Daimler and Benz companies amalgamated and adopted the laurel wreath and the three-pointed star as their new trademark.

Q —

Why are the front wheels of a tractor smaller than the back wheels?

A —

The front wheels are smaller to minimise tire contact with the ground and thus make steering easier. They also allow for tighter turning. The rear wheels are large to give maximum tire contact with the ground. This gives better stability and traction and also softens the ride somewhat for the driver in the absence of suspension.

Q —

What was the make of the car in the *Back to the Future* movies?

A —

The car was a DeLorean, made in Dunmurray just outside Belfast. About 9,200 cars were made during 1981 and 1982. The DeLorean is most famous for its gull-wing doors and stainless steel exterior.

Q —

Is there a difference between 'four-wheel drive' and 'all-wheel drive'?

A —

All-wheel drive vehicles have permanently engaged or automatically engaging four-wheel drive capability. Four-wheel drive means that the vehicle has manually engaging, temporary four-wheel drive capability.

Q —

Why are automobiles called cars?

A —

Believe it or not, the word car comes to us from Old Celtic 'karrom, karros' via Latin 'carrum' and Old Northern French 'carre', its underlying meaning being 'to move swiftly'.

Q —

Why is there always a copy of the Bible in hotel rooms?

A

Most bibles found in hotel rooms today are placed there by The Gideons, founded in Wisconsin in 1899. They are a Christian professional and businessmen's association and have 130,000 members in more than 170 countries. Many of the early Gideons were travelling salesmen who would leave a bible at the reception desk of any hotel they used so that other guests could borrow it. Today the Gideons place bibles in prisons, hospitals and military bases, as well as hotel rooms – more that 45 million annually! However, credit for starting this tradition has to go to the International Bible Society, which was founded in New York in 1809. They are a leading publisher of foreign language bibles, publishing in more than 350 languages. The I.B.S. donated bibles to soldiers during the American Civil War and started placing them in hotels as early as 1823.

Q ▬

Ray, is true that when you flush the toilet on the train it goes onto the tracks. Say it isn't so. Uuurrgh!
— Anne Marie, Listowel

The man who deals with all our rail-related queries is Iarnrod Eireann PRO Barry Kenny. So where does it go when we flush the toilet on the train, Barry?

 A —

In common with other railways around the world, all of the modern trains, certainly everything we've bought since 1994 have waste retention units and they are discharged regularly. However, prior to that all trains in Ireland and indeed internationally, would discharge the water from the toilets onto the track, where it drains away. And that is one of the reasons why there is a request not to use the toilet while trains are stopped at the stations.

 Q —

Ray, you know all the road signs telling how many people have been killed on the roads of certain counties over the last four years? What do the two numbers mean – why is one crossed out?
— Gemma, Carlow

It's probably the most popular question of Fix It Friday. *The man with the answer is the Senior Project Manager of Road Traffic Safety for the National Roads Association, Harry Cullen.*

A —

There are two different figures on the signs. If we take the year 2003 the top figure represents the number of people killed in car crashes between 1999 and 2002 inclusive. The figure underneath it displays the number of victims between 1998 and 2001 inclusive. The sign says 'the number of people killed in the last four years', therefore, for the sign to remain current, the number is updated every year. The idea behind the signs is to give people an indication of whether the figures are going up or down.

SONGS

After all his plastic surgery . . . do you reckon Michael Jackson could be the first solo artist to break up? — *Anon*

Is it true The Corrs are splitting up so they can spend more time with their family?
— *Martin, Drogheda*

Q —

What is the name of the castle on the cover of the U2 album *Unforgettable Fire*?

A —

It is Moydrum Castle in Co. Westmeath.

Q —

When did Michael Jackson play Cork? My dog was born that day and we called him Jack.

A —

Jacko played Páirc Uí Caoimh on 30th and 31st July 1988, which makes your dog a good age!

Q —

Where and when did the Eurovision Song Contest begin?

A —

Eurovision is the name of a Europe-wide TV distribution network established by the European Broadcasting Union in the mid-1950s. The Eurovision Song Contest was first held in

Switzerland in 1956. The contest is also open to countries outside of Europe, e.g. Israel, who are members of the EBU.

Q —

Did Andy Warhol design the Rolling Stones' famous lips?

A —

Andy Warhol did design the tongue and lips which are now the Rolling Stones' logo. He also designed the infamous *Sticky Fingers* album cover with the unzipping fly.

Q —

Are you going to tell me what a Buffalo Soldier is?

A —

Buffalo Soldiers, as sung about by the late Bob Marley, were former African slaves who fought with the US Army against the native American tribes. The native Americans gave them the name Buffalo Soldiers out of respect, after an animal which they considered sacred. It was a tribute to their fearlessness in battle and to their dark skin and thick, curly hair.

In the Marc Cohn song 'Walking in Memphis' what is the second line of the chorus, please?

It is 'walking with my feet ten feet off of Beale'. Beale Street in Memphis is famous for its blues music. It is one of Tennessee's top tourist destinations.

How many number one hits did the Beatles have?

The Fab Four had 17 UK Number Ones.

What was the Thin Lizzy number that was a *Top of the Pops* theme tune?

The number was 'Yellow Pearl'. It was actually performed by Phil Lynott and not Thin Lizzy. It featured on his solo album, *Solo in Soho*.

Q —

Did Bruce Springsteen play with the Traveling Wilburys?

A —

No. He did perform in concert with Roy Orbison and took part in a televised tribute to him. The Wilburys were Bob Dylan (Lucky), Jeff Lynne (Otis), Tom Petty (Charlie T. Jr), Roy Orbison (Lefty) and George Harrison (Nelson).

Q —

What is the biggest selling album of all time?

A —

Michael Jackson's *Thriller* with over 50 million copies sold worldwide.

Q —

What were U2 called before they became U2?

A

As teenage schoolboys they called themselves Feedback. They later became Hype and eventually U2.

Q —

Is there any difference between a fiddle and a violin?

A —

They are the same instrument – the difference is in the way they are played. The only slight difference in the structure of the instrument is sometimes seen in the bridge. Instruments played as violins usually have an arched bridge, allowing for easier bowing of a single string, and those played as fiddles tend to have a flattened bridge.

Q —

In the making of which music video did Simon Le Bon almost drown?

A —

Le Bon, lead singer with Duran Duran, had two close shaves with water. When making the video for 'Wild Boys' the windmill vane to which he was strapped became temporarily jammed, leaving him underwater. He was also involved in a serious incident in a coastal yacht race in 1985 in his own boat, *Drum*.

Q —

About which artist is the song 'Matchstalk Men'?

A —

L.S. Lowry, who painted everyday scenes of his hometown, Salford, near Manchester.

Q —

Why did British soldiers sing 'It's a long way to Tipperary'?

A —

The song was written in 1912 by Jack Judge and Harry Williams. The song is about an Irishman working in London and wishing himself back home in Tipperary. Its catchy tune made it a good marching song and it was taken to World War I by the Connaught Rangers. It stood the test of time and was also sung by soldiers in World War II.

Which popular song has been most frequently covered?

The most recorded popular song is 'Yesterday', written by Lennon & McCartney. It has been recorded by artists as diverse as Frank Sinatra, Benny Goodman, Foster & Allen, Marty Robbins, Liberace, Aled Jones, Vera Lynn and the Band of the Scots Guards – to name but a few!

Which Irish band had the single called 'The Bride Wore White'?

The Blades, fronted by Paul Cleary. It was one side of a double A-sided single, the other track being 'Animation'. It was released in March 1982.

Q —

What the hell is a 'pompatus of love' – as in the Steve Miller song 'The Joker'?

A —

Steve Miller used 'the pompatus of love' in his 1973 hit 'The Joker':

> Some people call me the space cowboy.
> Yeah! Some call me the gangster of love.
> Some people call me Maurice,
> Cause I speak of the pompatus of love.

Miller has said little about the P-word over the years. In at least one interview he claimed: 'it doesn't mean anything – it's just jive talk.'

This is not quite true. The lyric sounds rather like a line featured in 'The Letter' by the Medallions. The song had been a hit in R & B circles in 1954. It had the lines, 'Oh my darling, let me whisper sweet words of pizmotality and discuss the puppetutes of love.' Now there are two strange words to explain!!

The song had been written and sung by a member of the Medallions named Vernon Green and when he was tracked down he said he'd never even heard 'The Joker.' He laughed when he heard the song for the first time. Green says 'The Letter' was his attempt to conjure up his dream woman.

According to Green: 'Pizmotality described words of such secrecy that they could only be spoken to the one you loved. Puppetutes is a term I coined to mean a secret paper-doll fantasy figure who would be my everything and bear my children.' Perhaps a cross between a puppet and a prostitute. Not a very PC sentiment but it was 1954!!

So the story goes that Steve Miller misheard 'puppetutes' as 'pompatus' and the speculating began.